Charles R. Anderson, MLS
Peter Sprenkle, MLS

Reference Librarianship
Notes from the Trenches

Pre-publication
REVIEWS,
COMMENTARIES,
EVALUATIONS . . .

"When did Anderson and Sprenkle work at my reference desk? The issues the authors raise in this informative work deal with the day-to-day problems a frontline librarian faces, no matter what type of library he or she may work in. Informative essays deal with the library as the source of all information, technology innovations, the evolution from the library as the people's university to social service center, and staffing the library of the future. Complementing the essays are Web log entries depicting typical shifts on a reference desk. For every library user who needs help finding information, there are many others who want to borrow a pencil, pen, paper, or stapler; need to find the restroom; sign up for the Internet; require assistance with a computer freeze or crash, paper jam in the printer or copier; or want tax forms. This book is for every practicing librarian who needs reassurance that he or she is not alone, as well as students seeking to find out what the profession is really about."

Sue Kamm, MLS
Acting Head, Branch Library Services,
Inglewood Public Library,
Inglewood, California

More pre-publication
REVIEWS, COMMENTARIES, EVALUATIONS . . .

"**T**his book should be required reading for anyone who works or wants to work in any type of library—for reference people to learn that they are not alone, and everyone else to understand how difficult dealing with the public can be. I intend to make everyone I work with read my copy."

Laura Blalock, MSIS
Electronic Services and Reference Librarian,
Tennessee Technological University

"**T**his book combines a thoughtful presentation of issues facing today's reference librarian with a blow-by-blow account of life at the reference desk."

Patricia Groh, MLS
Coordinator of Community Services,
Skokie Public Library

"**N**o doubt librarians who receive this book as a gift will place it in the bathroom magazine rack, on the night stand, or on the table in the library's staff lounge to be sampled, bit by bit. Each time they open the book, they'll nod knowingly when they recognize archetypical patron behaviors and laugh, and shake their heads, and smile. Readers in library school will gain insight into the reality of being a 'grunt' at the public library reference desk and their instructors will find practice reference questions and scenarios for their students. Retirees will discover that things have stayed the same as much as they have changed."

Tara Severns, MLS
Associate Professor-Librarian,
Windward Community College Library

"**R**eference Librarianship: Notes from the Trenches should be required reading for any library school student who's considering public library work. The dichotomy of a grunt's diary interspersed with commentary and musings from an illustrious reference librarian and administrator begs the longstanding question, 'Is librarianship an occupation or a profession?' From policy questions to collection management to 'libraries as place,' this book will make you think twice about where we've been and where we're going. Anderson and Sprenkle will help guide you through the trenches."

Shelley Voie, MLS
Reference Librarian,
King County Library System

The Haworth Information Press®
An Imprint of The Haworth Press
New York • London • Oxford

NOTES FOR PROFESSIONAL LIBRARIANS AND LIBRARY USERS

This is an original book title published by The Haworth Information Press®, an imprint of The Haworth Press, Inc. Unless otherwise noted in specific chapters with attribution, materials in this book have not been previously published elsewhere in any format or language.

CONSERVATION AND PRESERVATION NOTES

All books published by The Haworth Press, Inc., and its imprints are printed on certified pH neutral, acid-free book grade paper. This paper meets the minimum requirements of American National Standard for Information Sciences-Permanence of Paper for Printed Material, ANSI Z39.48-1984.

DIGITAL OBJECT IDENTIFIER (DOI) LINKING

The Haworth Press is participating in reference linking for elements of our original books. (For more information on reference linking initiatives, please consult the CrossRef Web site at www.crossref.org.) When citing an element of this book such as a chapter, include the element's Digital Object Identifier (DOI) as the last item of the reference. A Digital Object Identifier is a persistent, authoritative, and unique identifier that a publisher assigns to each element of a book. Because of its persistence, DOIs will enable The Haworth Press and other publishers to link to the element referenced, and the link will not break over time. This will be a great resource in scholarly research.

Reference Librarianship
Notes from the Trenches

THE HAWORTH INFORMATION PRESS®

New, Recent, and Forthcoming Titles of Related Interest

Computers in Libraries: An Introduction for Library Technicians
by Katie Wilson

Puzzles and Essays from "The Exchange": Tricky Reference Questions
by Charles R. Anderson

Libraries and Google^{SM} edited by William Miller and Rita M. Pellen

New Directions in Reference edited by Byron Anderson and Paul Webb

Reference Librarianship
Notes from the Trenches

Charles R. Anderson, MLS
Peter Sprenkle, MLS

The Haworth Information Press®
An Imprint of The Haworth Press
New York • London • Oxford

For more information on this book or to order, visit
http://www.haworthpress.com/store/product.asp?sku=5672

or call 1-800-HAWORTH (800-429-6784) in the United States and Canada
or (607) 722-5857 outside the United States and Canada

or contact orders@HaworthPress.com

Published by

The Haworth Information Press®, an imprint of The Haworth Press, Inc., 10 Alice Street, Binghamton, NY 13904-1580.

All cartoons created by Jeremy Smith.

PUBLISHER'S NOTE
The development, preparation, and publication of this work has been undertaken with great care. However, the Publisher, employees, editors, and agents of The Haworth Press are not responsible for any errors contained herein or for consequences that may ensue from use of materials or information contained in this work. The Haworth Press is committed to the dissemination of ideas and information according to the highest standards of intellectual freedom and the free exchange of ideas. Statements made and opinions expressed in this publication do not necessarily reflect the views of the Publisher, Directors, management, or staff of The Haworth Press, Inc., or an endorsement by them.

Cover design by Jennifer M. Gaska.

Library of Congress Cataloging-in-Publication Data

Anderson, Charles R., 1935-
  Reference librarianship : notes from the trenches / Charles R. Anderson, Peter Sprenkle.
    p. cm.
  Includes bibliographical references (p.) and index.
  ISBN-13: 978-0-7890-2947-8 (hc. : alk. paper)
  ISBN-10: 0-7890-2947-2 (hc. : alk. paper)
  ISBN-13: 978-0-7890-2948-5 (pbk. : alk. paper)
  ISBN-10: 0-7890-2948-0 (pbk. : alk. paper)
  1. Reference services (Libraries). 2. Sprenkle, Peter—Weblogs. 3. Reference librarians—Weblogs. 4. Public libraries—Reference services—United States. 5. Reference librarians—Effect of technological innovations on. 6. Internet in library reference services. 7. Libraries and the Internet. 8. Libraries—Public opinion. 9. Libraries—Forecasting. 10. Libraries—Humor. I. Sprenkle, Peter. II. Title.

Z711.A394 2006
025.5'2—dc22

                                                        2005034843

To everyone who works with the public.

ABOUT THE AUTHORS

Charles R. Anderson, MLS, has been a reference librarian for thirty years, serving in libraries from the East Coast to the Midwest to the Northwest. During his library career he has published extensively in library literature and has contributed chapters to books on reference services with emphasis on the effects of computer applications. From 1984 to 1999 he edited the column, "The Exchange" in *RQ* (later *RUSQ*), the official journal of the Reference and User Services Division of the American Library Association. His most recent book was *Puzzles and Essays from "The Exchange": Tricky Reference Questions* (Haworth).

Peter Sprenkle, MLS, has worked as a reference librarian in a large public library for thirteen years. In 2003, he began a Web log called "Ref Grunt," in which he listed every desk transaction that came to him. The Web log was retired in May 2004, but is added to from time to time.

CONTENTS

Preface

Professional journals in the field of librarianship offer theoretical and sometimes even practical advice about many aspects of being a reference librarian. Fine books on reference work have been written, such as Celia Hales Mabry's *Doing the Work of Reference: Practical Tips for Excelling As a Reference Librarian* (Mabry, 2001) and Bill Katz's classic *Introduction to Reference Work* (Katz, 1992).

Despite these excellent guides, little published information gets down to the level of what it is like now to spend day after day working in the reference "trench lines." For this reason, we have gathered and arranged in the form of a diary the contents of a yearlong project that recorded actual reference-desk encounters. A young reference librarian in a Midwest library, using the pseudonym "Ref Grunt," an allusion to the infantry soldier's appellation of "Grunt," posted these transactions daily to an online blog (Web log). These blogs are published here in unexpurgated form (except for the deletion of approximately 50 percent of the listings out of space concerns).

Interspersed with the monthly diaries are essays inspired by issues raised in the blogs and in various online discussion groups. These essays, intended to raise questions for debate rather than answer them, were written by a now-retired reference librarian who began working in libraries in the days when a computer meant a mainframe programmed by IBM (Hollerith) punch cards, and the primary online database was ERIC (Educational Resources Information Center), accessed by a massive line printer about three feet wide with no monitor. Thirty years later this author oversaw the systemwide use of networked catalog and Internet access through fiber connections.

Our purpose in offering this material is to paint a clear picture of the field for library and information science students, to provide emotional and philosophical support for practitioners of reference librarianship (You are not alone!), and, finally, to remind library administrators of what life is like for a grunt in the reference trench lines.

Reference Librarianship: Notes from the Trenches
© 2006 by The Haworth Press, Inc. All rights reserved.
doi:10.1300/5672_a

Chapter 1

Directional Questions

"JUST POINT ME TO THE . . ."

Early in my library career, I became an untutored student of human behavior. An observation made by a customer sparked this interest. The person stopped me as I was bustling toward the reference desk. She said, "You must work here—you are moving so fast!" Later that day her comment came back to me and I realized that, with probably 95 percent certainty, one could tell the customers from the staff in a strange library by the speed with which the respective parties moved. Most customers, unless they are very frequent visitors, sort of wander around, gazing for helpful landmarks. Library staff members, who (in most cases) know where they are going, are able to move much faster.

As an aside, another customer observation gave me a clue in the area of job function recognition. This remark came when I worked in a third-level reference referral operation. Because I did not have any public desk duties and frequently spent a lot of time on the floor of the reference stacks poring through books or in the basement environs among dusty old library materials, I often wore jeans to work. This customer started to ask me a question and then said, "Oh, I'm sorry, I realize you're not a librarian." Since she was looking directly at my clothing, I concluded that because I did not fit her stereotype of a librarian, she made a judgment call based on what communication experts call the "halo effect."

To get back to how users find their way around in a library, we have to address the whole issue of "signage." Signage has been a subject of serious study in library literature, with the results applied in varying practical fashions from "Forget it" to "You cannot get around for stumbling over the signs." Americans are particularly fond of signs.

doi:10.1300/5672_01

I noticed this upon returning from a trip to England. The British are more restrained than we are about signs. I did notice charming examples such as the one on the inside of a gentlemen's (men's room) door in London. It read, "Gentlemen, please remember to adjust your trousers." How genteel a way to remind one not to exit the restroom unzipped. The "Curb Your Dog" sign I saw in London took me a few moments to deduce it was not some bizarre suggestion to mistreat your dog, but rather to ensure that any mess produced by your dog ended up in the area between the sidewalk and the street. Furthermore, after a bit of observation I realized the clear implication was that one should perform an action frequently ignored in this country, that is, pick up your dog's droppings. When I got back to the States, the plethora of signs after three weeks of visual signatory deprivation almost resulted in a case of cognitive dissonance.

What are the techniques that customers in our over-signed world use to find things in our libraries? It seems to me that objects with an external (to the library) existence are no problem, while things that generally appear only in libraries are practically invisible to users. Take, for example, pencil sharpeners. In one library, we had a pencil sharpener mounted on top of some vertical files. The pencil sharpener was about thirty feet from the reference desk. When someone asked, "Where is the pencil sharpener" it often took just a slight nod in the direction of the top of those vertical files and the customer was off like a shot to use the sharpener. However, to get someone to a display of tax forms (something that library customers fortunately do not encounter every day), although located less than twenty feet from the reference desk, we often had to lead the person to the display. After hundreds of treks to the display every hour during tax season, we finally put red feet stickers down on the rug leading from the desk to the display. This worked admirably, but the feet did tend to collect a lot of dirt!

As a measure of how well library signage works, one might look at the number of "directional" questions that come to a reference desk. In 1993, I was responsible for a study of reference/directional questions in a large library system. The questions that were directional in nature ranged from 11 to 60 percent, with no clear correlation between the size of the library and the result. No effort was ever made to compare these results with physical layouts in each library, presumably because the existing arrangements were fixed and additional signage was not a high priority. A cursory examination of similar studies in library literature, as well as "common knowledge," does confirm the importance of dealing with these directional questions, since they do tend to make up a somewhat significant percent of reference desk encounters. This fact alone would seem to be an argument for good, detailed signage. After all, one vital dictum that some libraries seem to forget is Ranganathan's Fourth Law of Library Science, "Save the time of the reader."

As an early reader, although it has been more than fifty years, I still remember the Carnegie library that formed an important element in my youth. Just the appearance of the library sent a message of serious purpose, although entertainment in the form of novels was also valued. When you walked into the main reading room you saw a long counter on the left where you checked out *books*—not magazines, not CDs, not videotapes, not DVDs, not stuffed animals, not tools—none of the myriad materials that libraries offer today. Directly ahead was a small desk with someone seated at it that you knew immediately to be a "librarian," someone to go to if you needed help.

Contrast that to the modern library. Architecturally driven design elements, which may or may not be comprehensible to users of varying backgrounds, take the place of content-driven signage. To illustrate, I recently visited a rather large library that years ago focused on the provision of information services, when it had an extensive print reference collection and a visually prominent reference desk. Now, once you go through the security gate, your eye is drawn to a free-standing display of "Hot Stuff!" almost directly ahead. To the right are study tables and chairs. Barely visible through a narrow lane, somewhat blocked by these chairs, is a little desk, backed by a few shelves of reference materials, with a small sign reading "Information." To the left is a small food court/café, with about the most visible signage in the entire library offering Munch Ease [sic], Hot Beverages, and [presumably cold] Beverages. At least a new library visitor should be in no doubt about the relative importance of various library offerings. It would be interesting to compare the percentage of directional questions in the new, architectural-award-winning libraries with pre-facelift statistics.

For readers old enough to remember giants of the reference field such as Louis Shores, it is easy to picture these progenitors, driven by the mission of making information available to the public, rumbling restlessly in their no doubt book-lined crypts. However, we are told, based on somewhat selective and directed surveys, that the public wants libraries to be more like commercial book stores, coffee shops, Internet cafés, and community centers. If this is true, it seems to me a sad commentary on a public that has been seduced by sound bites, fast food, and intellectually limited thought patterns.

📖 📖 📖

A GRUNT'S DIARY: MAY-JUNE 2003

Wednesday, May 14, 2003

In the Afternoon

Checked to see if an Internet terminal was set up.

Directions to a place in a nearby city.

"High school books in Spanish."

"Where is 'B FRA?'"" (In the biographies. I forget the subject's name).

"You have a garbage can?" (Yes we do.)

A request for today's local paper.

Steam locomotive engine diagrams. He insisted that a physics book would have them.

A child's ailment called "Gerb."

A man showed me a business card. "You know where this is?" We found out.

"Can you send this via e-mail for me?" He couldn't quite grasp the concept of having an account.

A request for *"Value Line,"* which we keep behind the desk.

Timelines for World Wars I and II. Timelines would be a recurring request.

The Sunday paper.

Two books by Rita Williams-Garcia. If I was a young adult I wouldn't be able to figure out our YA section either.

Baby name books.

In the Evening

Inventions between 1910 and 1919. Yup, it's that time of the year again, when middle schoolers are assigned a decade to research for an essay.

"Where are your history books?" She actually wanted timelines.

Books about the 1940s. More timelines.

Books about the *Titanic*.

Twins magazine. I have never heard of it.

"Entrepreneurs, like Puff Daddy."

Her friend wanted books on Michael Jordan, but changed her mind and asked for books on the Holocaust.

Today's paper.

Botany books.

Today's paper.

An eight year-old told us that the library had a leak.

Tuck Everlasting.

"Can I use your phone?" No. Ask the circ desk.

Salvador Dali.

A Mark Twain impersonator came in looking for a childhood friend.

Advice on using the printer.

Books on Caligula. We only had one in the biographies. I suggested he also look at Roman history books. He didn't know why.

Books on Australia. That assignment was due a couple days ago, I think. Tsk.

Internet signups: 23

Times I had to deal with the copy machine's bad button: 4

Friday, May 16, 2003

In the Morning

"Can you sharpen this?"

"Where's the bathroom?"

Sorry, sir. The computers can't handle that kind of disk.

Click the green button. Yeah, that one there.

Come into My Trading Room, by Alexander Elder. I sent off an ILL request. Hope I spelled the customer's name right.

"Can I borrow your pen?"

An Internet terminal crashes.

Printing advice.

They can make change at the circ desk.

"Where is (another librarian)?"

"Grant books are over here, right?"

Someone donated a big bag of old videos.

Long conversation about our debit card system.

Consumer Reports for lawn mowers.

Another donation—this one is cash!

How to Cure Yourself of Positive Thinking, by Donald G. Smith.

"I need that form again." (We have several form books with hundreds of forms.)

Coin prices

In the Afternoon

Books about Walt Whitman.

"I got to learn how to use the computers one of these days. You know, I'm still used to the old fashioned card catalog etc., etc." He wanted books on woodworking.

Stapler? Right here, Ma'am.

A book with all the broadcasters in it.

Spanish for Gringos.

"I lost my library card."

Printer advice.

Newspaper.

Pencil.

An experiment with two-sided copying turns out badly.

Newspaper.

"Can I use this pencil?"

Train schedules.

Printer instruction.

Books on leadership.

"Do books with long call numbers go in a special place?"

The Barefoot Contessa Cookbook.

More leadership books.

Sir, the library is closing. We need you to take the books to the circ desk to check them out. . . . Sir, we're closed. . . . Sir? . . . Sir?

Internet signups: 61

Bad button help: 1

Monday, May 19, 2003

In the Morning

Printer help.

"Why did only 12 scrambled words come up? I wanted 20." I never did figure out what she was talking about.

You need a period after the www, ma'am.

It's spelled T-I-E.

A public terminal crashed.

"What's the number to the vehicle emission testing station?" Maybe if I had put the phone book in the right place it wouldn't have taken so long to answer.

You need to type @ after your username, sir.

A gentleman hands me his ID, yet I ask him his name. Why do I do this?

"How do you alphabetize a list in Excel?"

Lucky, by Alice Sebold. Later she asked for other books on rape victims.

Computer crash.

Computer crash.

Computer crash.

Scissors.

Print server crash.

Pencil.

Social Security, by Andrew Bergman, the search interrupted three times by computer crashes.

"How do I get a blank page to come up in Word?"

Computer crash.

"I need some copies made."

Dictionaries.

"Antrim," by Robinson Jeffers. Hello, Grangers!

Computer crash.

Computer crash.

Computer crash.

Computer crash.

Resumé formatting.

Copy machine advice.

In the Afternoon

Pencil.

Pencil.

Network down.

I tell people that I can't sign them up for an Internet terminal because the network is down, and they just stand there, staring into space.

One of them asks for three days worth of newspapers.

Microfiche machine explanation.

Funny You Should Ask, by Marvin Terban.

Sorry, sir, the network is still down. (Multiply by twenty and insert randomly into the remainder of the day.)

Magic tricks, but he pretty much already knew where they are.

One of our large interior plate glass windows shattered, just shattered. No one was hurt and it made a fascinating noise, like a crystal waterfall landing on soil.

"Books on prostitution; you know, whores?"

Blue Book prices.

"Do you have PowerPoint?"

Someone from the county called to ask if any criminal activity had occurred on a particular street. Someone else referred her to us. She was dubious, with good reason.

Books on the 1950s.

Basement remodeling books.

"Math puzzles." Okay. I show him the books.

"Just math." Certainly. I show him the books.

"I need them in Spanish." Grr . . .

Almanac.

The Way Meat Loves Salt, by Nina Jaffe.

Maya Angelou books.

The Guardian, by Nicholas Sparks.

Internet requests: 44

Bad copier button: 1

Wednesday, May 21, 2003

In the Afternoon

Printer advice.

A customer with fines was mistakenly referred to us.

Printer advice.

Looking for *Antwone Fisher*, which another customer told us was actually called *Finding Fisher*.

The other customer became entranced with public service and tried to give a customer printer advice.

Stapler. It was empty.

Printer advice.

Printer advice.

"Is this the circulation desk?"

Phone number to the unemployment office.

Today's paper.

In the Evening

Faeries, by Brian Froud.

Her printer crashed at home. She needed to print out an e-mail. I could not guarantee success.

Three books not on the shelf because they are in the children's section.

Frida, by Hayden Herrera.

A Child Called It, by David J. Pelzer.

Empire, by Niall Ferguson.

Books on abortion, but the kid's English was so poor I was unable to narrow down the question.

Pencil.

"Who invented television, and in what year?"

"My boyfriend's brother is in jail, and I want to find out why."

Location of a college.

Fish illustrations.

Info on this town. He rejected everything I showed him.

Where a college was, and driving directions.

Restroom.

Putting a border in a Microsoft Word document.

"Books on Haiti. Yeah, Haiti. And Voodoo."

Part of the Net is down, but not all.

Sorry, we can't do double-sided copies.

Another with a troublesome accent. All I understood was the word "energy."

Pregnancy and childbirth books.

Two different printer problems.

Sheet music to the *Mission: Impossible* theme.

"Do you have any Macs?" Sorry.

"How about Zip drives?" I disappoint the nice lady again.

2001 tax forms.

Books on substitute teaching.

Algebra books. She later changed the request to fractions.

Colored pencils.

"Books, good books, on the Forties."

"Good books on the Holocaust. With lots of pictures."

Book sales.

Our print network defeats another customer.

Map and driving directions to San Diego.

Getting Your Child from No to Yes: Without Nagging, Bribing, or Threatening, by Jerry Wyckoff. We didn't have that, but we did have *Discipline Without Shouting or Spanking,* by the same author.

Internet signups: 11 (there were many more)

Tuesday, May 27, 2003

In the Morning

"When is your tax support workshop?" They stopped after April 15.

The Devil Wears Prada, by Lauren Weisberger.

A Cold Heart, by Jonathan Kellerman.

No Second Chance, by Harlan Coben.

Rental ordinances.

Young adult books.

"I need these printed out." The printer is down.

Newspaper.

"Tax form. That one there, that says '02."

The printer is down, sir.

Yesterday's paper.

Absolutely, ma'am, you could print out your resumé here, however . . .

Computer crash.

A periodical called *Cat Cat Cat.*

A book called *Cat Cat Cat?*

A corporation called Cat Cat Cat?

ADD books in Spanish.

Red Book (this Red Book is for medical supply companies).

Yesterday's paper.

In the Afternoon

Queen Bees & Wannabes, by Rosalind Wiseman

School financial aid forms.

Executive Power, by Vince Flynn.

The Web is still partly down, and our customers despair.

A gentleman hands us some partly filled-out ILL forms.

Explanation of Internet use rules.

Books on reserve are at the other desk, sir.

The Guardian, by Nicholas Sparks.

Directions to the courthouse.

Yesterday's paper.

Bus schedules.

"We're moving to town and need some information. . . ."

A. D. McGuire books.

Sidney Sheldon books.

More directions.

Free map.

The Testament, by John Grisham.

Books about a nearby town.

Books on electroplating.

Clipping file on a local landmark.

Los Seis Pilares de la Autoestima, by Nathaniel Branden.

40 Songs for a Better World (actually she only needed one song).

Books translated by Sigrid Undset.

Internet signups: 42

Wednesday, May 28, 2003

In the Evening

Horoscope books.

Real estate books.

Adult literacy books.

A library fine question that shouldn't have come to us.

1999-2001 high school yearbooks.

Books on the Nineties.

Divorce handbook, with forms on disk.

Books on carpentry projects, I think.

Ultra Black Hair Growth II: Another 6" Longer 1 Year from Now, by Cathy Howse.

"Where is Adult Fiction?"

Books on the Nineties. Being out, I show him books on the twentieth century. "That would have the Nineties in it?"

"Poem books," for her "poem class."

"Sports of the 1990s." The same brain-dead kids.

The poem girl returns.

"I'm looking for two girls that came here."

The carpentry guy comes in.

Mark Twain biographies.

"Where are the kids' books?"

Printer advice.

Internet woes.

Friday's paper, which I could not locate, allowing the customer to sigh righteously over our incompetence.

"Are you a notary?"

Books on the Holocaust.

Fetal development.

The names of our senators. (The customer's going to take the citizenship exam.)

"Revenge Waves in Unprotected Waters," by Anne Tyler. The kid needed this short story by tomorrow, but I could not find an anthology that had it. I managed to locate it in a 1977 issue of *The New Yorker,* but the microfiche reader died after we had printed page one.

Internet signups: 4

Wednesday, June 04, 2003

In the Morning

A computer crash to start my day.

Paper clip.

Directions.

Summer reading club.

Festival schedule.

CDs.

Printer advice.

Mad About Mia, about Millie Criswell.

Press conference? What press conference?

Printer problem.

"Book, pre-Christ to 1700, like Nefertiti."

"Where are the people to fill out your tax forms?"

'91 Mazda 323 repair manual.

Pen.

If You Want to Be Rich & Happy, Don't Go to School?, by Robert T. Kiyosaki.

The floppy disk is in the A: drive, sir.

Staple remover.

"Where are your photocopiers?"

Stapler.

Art of War, by Sun Tzu.

Newspaper microfilm.

In the Evening

Resumé books.

Missing wallet is found.

How to Get into the Top Law Schools, by Richard Montauk.

Books listing campgrounds.

Baby names.

"Typewriter?" Sorry.

Immigration forms we don't have.

Robinson Crusoe, by Daniel Defoe (unabridged).

Children's books.

Printing advice.

All in a Lifetime, by Ruth K. Westheimer.

Children's nonfiction.

Sheet music: "L'Amour-Toujours-L'Amour."

Bathroom.

"Can these be checked out?" No.

Help with the finicky printer.

A description of our databases.

Computer signups: 6

Tuesday, June 10, 2003

In the Morning

Don't run! (This to a staff member)

Newspaper.

Newspaper.

Interlibrary loan follow-up.

Classified ads.

Interlibrary loan followup.

Printing advice.

More Microsoft Works hassles.

Article from the June 9 *Fortune.*

Computer crash.

Computer crash.

Computer crash.

How to copy a floppy.

Family Development: Empowering Families to Move Out of Poverty, by Arlene McAtee.

In the Afternoon

Computer crash (mine).

Yearbooks.

Book club.

Books by Suzanne Brockman, and an online catalog demonstration.

Children scream. A woman rolls her eyes. "Yes, they are mine."

FAFSA forms.

American Life, by Madonna.

Internet workshop schedule request.

Scissors.

The Rights of Desire, by André Philippus Brink.

Spanish grammar books.

A customer and I are discussing the graphic novel series *Preacher.* A second customer chimes in. It becomes a theological debate.

Mosby's Textbook for Nursing Assistants, 2000 edition, by Sheila Sorrentino.

Ryan White Act subcommittee testimony.

A customer asks about a hold. She has the wrong library.

Stapler.

Internet signups: 36

Thursday, June 12, 2003

In the Morning

Weight Watchers "points."

Printer Advice.

New *King James Study Bible.*

Book suggestion: *Be Careful Who You SLAPP.*

Public Relations: The Profession and the Practice, by Otis W. Baskin and Craig E. Aronoff.

Printer advice.

Books on Adobe Photo Deluxe.

"Sixth-sense books, and I think it's called metaphysics."

SAT writing practice book.

PDR.

Computer workshop question.

"Any books on (I didn't quite get it) Acupas (Acappas?), kind of a witch, on Scooby-Doo?"

English for Russian speakers.

The Lake House, by James Patterson.

Light in Shadow, by Jayne Ann Krentz.

The Da Vinci Code, by Dan Brown.

"Any job openings?"

In the Afternoon

Microfilm reader help.

"Medical terminology."

N.A.D.A.

"Do you send faxes here?"

She wanted me to list our entire computer class schedule, day by day, over the phone. I'm mailing her a schedule instead.

"Where are the mysteries, you know, the fun books?" Later she came back and asked for books about serial killers.

Sign language books.

Printer advice.

Dictionary.

Consumer Reports: Camcorders.

"Fax machine?" When I said a place next door would fax for a dollar, she got upset.

Phone book.

Bruce Lee books.

Another fax machine request.

Children's books.

Internet signups: 36

Friday, June 20, 2003

In the Morning

Lost ID.

Old newspaper microfilm.

"Are you open Sundays?"

"I need the Internet. I don't know how to work it." Oh, god.

Printer advice.

Divorce books.

Printer advice.

Value Line.

White and yellow pages.

Yesterday's paper.

Bathroom.

"Paperbacks?"

Home organization businesses in the area.

Art of War, by Sun Tzu.

N.A.D.A. used car price guide.

The Bark Canoes and Skin Boats of North America, by Edwin Tappan Adney, and Howard I. Chapelle.

The Winds of War, by Herman Wouk.

Fire insurance maps.

Our address.

What Makes Juries Listen Now, by Sonya Hamlin.

In the Afternoon

The GED is now harder. Do we have the new exam books?

A woman was herding her child, if that makes any sense.

My Bloody Life: The Making of a Latin King, by Reymundo Sanchez.

Books on gang culture.

"Did you get the fax I sent?" No.

Who stole our box of tissue?

Microfilm advice.

"A computer is like a car with a lot of electrical gadgets. When they work, it's great, but when they don't, it's a pain in the ass. I don't have a computer, and I don't have anything electrical in my car except the lights. I had mechanical windows and the rain started and the water got in and I had to drive all the way with the window open." This lecture delivered while we downloaded and printed out a tax form for the gentleman. Then we had to teach him how to use the copier.

Today's paper.

Loan officer exam books.

Medical career books. The woman can't settle on a career.

The Towers of the Sunset, by L. E. Modesitt Jr.

Crossroads of Twilight, by Robert Jordan.

Half of the customers coming to the desk are loonies. Well, it is Friday afternoon.

Roadrunner, by Trisha R. Thomas.

Painting books.

How to get to another city.

Internet signups: 41

Friday, June 27, 2003

In the Morning

Bankruptcy, chapter 7, not 13.

He lost his portfolio. Then he found it.

A customer wishes to know if he returned a book.

Microfilm advice.

Pencil and paper.

The other librarian on duty (Call her "Librarian Y") got a customer who wanted the Internet but had never used it before. Librarian Y suggested that she do the searching. He agreed. What would you like? "Sex," he replied. What about sex? "Porn." Never before had a customer asked us to download porn before! When we told him no, he asked for "revolutionary tracts," which in this case meant books on munitions and changing identity.

Today's paper.

The New Illustrated Science and Invention Encyclopedia, ed. Mark K. Datford.

He can't save the document he had slaved over because the A: drive is broken.

Printing advice.

Nearby papers.

Another A: drive problem.

Printer crash.

In the Afternoon

"I'm looking for a book by Dante . . . *The Comedy?*

Internet policy over the phone.

"Can I make copies of pictures in books?"

Librarian W and I share police run-in anecdotes.

Books on seamanship. Neither of us could remember the word, so I looked for "boat handling."

Pen.

A cop wants Stephen King books.

Landscaping books in Spanish.

Stapler.

Great Expectations, by Charles Dickens. This was a phone call from another library. They were ashamed to admit they didn't own a copy!

Is There a Loch Ness Monster? by Gerald S. Snyder.

"I need the Yahoo."

Fax machine.

Hulk: The Incredible Guide.

A man recovers his lost floppy disk.

Internet signups: 21

Chapter 2

The Library Has Everything

"ALICE'S RESTAURANT" OR "DO YOU HAVE . . ."

One of the most touching and at the same time most frustrating feature of public library reference work is the implicit faith people have that the library will possess in its environs anything and everything from the commonplace to the bizarre. To paraphrase the line in "Alice's Restaurant," (Arlo Guthrie), "You can get anything you want at your local library."

I am not talking here about the common questions that come up at a reference desk such as "Do you have a pen . . . a pencil . . . a pencil and paper . . . a pencil sharpener?" In an actual tally done by the authors, these specific questions accounted for approximately 11 percent of the customer contacts at the reference desk. Nor do we mean the repetitive "Where's the restroom?" requests. The older member of our author team remembers this as an extremely frequent question in the "old days." Now, however, for whatever reason—people's bladders are more resistant, more restrooms are available in public places nowadays, or perhaps the library signs for the restroom are more intelligible—the frequency of this previously desperate question has dropped. The tally of bathroom questions in a year accounted for only 2 percent of the total.

No, we are talking about less common items such as:

- a laminating machine
- immigration forms
- a lost ID
- middle school textbooks
- Pell Grant forms

Reference Librarianship: Notes from the Trenches
© 2006 by The Haworth Press, Inc. All rights reserved.
doi:10.1300/5672_02

- tax assessments
- tax brochures
- rental ordinances
- math tutors
- the pager I left here yesterday
- a fax machine
- college application forms
- aquarium passes
- a notary public
- bus schedules

To complicate matters further, news personnel on radio and television have the frustrating propensity to announce blithely, when reporting on some new civic study, official form, or how to sign up for some local event that, "You can get a copy at your local library" (of course never actually checking with the library to see if this is true).

Not only are the news media guilty of this, but often, the people who come in expecting something we do not have were told we did by a clueless city official. Although an optimist might theorize that these cases are a result of faith in public libraries, I suspect many outsiders direct people to the library not because they are certain of its contents, but because they want to get rid of an annoyance by sending them to us.

Sometimes what a customer expects us to have is reasonable. One library may not have a scanner, but some do. The same applies to notary public services, laminating machines, school textbooks, or a fax service. However, the reality is that not every library has everything— which of course is the source of much disappointment to the customer and frustration to the library staff.

I have always maintained that standing behind or under a sign reading "Information," "Reference," or, even worse, "Ask me" is one of the most stressful occupations in the world. There you are, all alone behind a desk, proudly proclaiming to the entire world that you can find the answer to anything you may be asked. Moreover, you are expected to keep doing this for hours at a time! To make matters worse, just when you are geared up in a really hot "I can find the answer to that" frame of mind, you find instead that the next person in front of you simply wants to know where the newspaper is, whether you have a paper clip he or she can borrow (who returns paper clips?), or informs you that an Internet terminal is down.

In considering the reasons for this generalized belief on the part of the public that the public library is a source for anything under the sun, I have concluded that it dates back to very early contacts with a library. Whether it was the first visit that your grade school class made to a library or even going further back to the "pre-school" story hour, somehow each person's young psyche, perhaps overwhelmed with the surroundings, was imprinted with a belief that the library had everything.

Remember, a small child's view of the world is quite different from an adult's perception. You might try this experiment at home: Get down on your hands and knees, at least below tabletop height. Crawl around and see all the different things that become visible. You can see the underside of tables, for example. In a library, a child at this height probably will see some interesting or disgusting things stuck to the underside of tables. More importantly, the vast height of book-shelves has to be very impressive to someone viewing them from a two- to three-foot height. The perspective given to a long row of shelves from this short height would add to the sense of limitless vistas. The library's books probably seem to stretch on forever and up to the sky. Hopefully, positive contacts with reference librarians increase the sense of library omnipotence. Of course, occasional blips may occur in this positive experience. I still remember the grade school librarian who made me feel stupid when giving a book report for *Twenty Thousand Leagues Under the Sea*. I did not know what a league was and opined that it was how deep the submarine went. The sarcastic response from this school librarian may have poisoned my feelings for librarians until I married one. All of this early indoctrination to the world of books has to have some significant aftereffects, even if only on a subconscious level.

What is most interesting to consider, given the Internet age and the impact this has made on young people's use of the library, is whether today's children have the same perception of public libraries. Although homework help is still a necessary part of our services, particularly as school libraries tend to close their doors when school is dismissed, observations from the field suggest some significant differences in the way children use libraries now than the way they did ten to twenty years ago.

One problem noted in conversations with librarians is the influx of kids, some latchkey, perhaps, who are primarily interested in playing computer games and checking e-mail. Will these children have the faith that today's adults do in the library as the ultimate source for everything? It may be difficult for library-sponsored programs that attempt to foster support and appreciation of the riches found in libraries to compete with Web browsing and e-mail. By the time these children of are voting age and computers are even more ubiquitous than they are today, will they be as willing to support libraries as voters today seem to be?

A GRUNT'S DIARY: JULY 2003

Thursday, July 03, 2003

In the Morning

Computer crash.

Extensive printer advice.

I print out a document for a sight-impaired customer.

Change for a dollar? Other desk.

She left her disk here yesterday.

Crime Partners, by Donald Goines.

Ladies room.

Internet crash.

You need an adult library card to use the computers, ma'am.

Printer advice.

Printer advice.

Yellow pages.

Printer advice.

He needs an obituary but the year he needs is not indexed.

Pep Boys' phone number.

Internet crash.

Windows' multiple screens confuse a customer.

Internet crash.

Word processor advice I am not qualified to give.

Tuesday's paper.

Book club.

Local historical photos. She then wanted to discuss them at length.

Directions to the kids section.

Pen.

Nine Anne Rice novels on tape.

The Lake House, by James Patterson.

In the Afternoon

It was a quiet shift, so I told Librarian X and Librarian Y all about last night's dream, where I was not only naked in public but flying at the time.

"Do you have books on CD?"

Book club.

Boys, stop hitting each other.

Today's paper didn't arrive again.

Books in Spanish.

Automatic transmission repair.

Cockatiels.

Anatomy.

Citizenship exam books.

Book club.

"Human behavior" was the closest she could narrow it down to, but she found some stuff.

Hunger of Memory: The Education of Richard Rodriguez, by Richard Rodriguez.

"Ingles basico?"

Internet signups: 35

Thursday, July 10, 2003

In the Morning

There's a spider lurking over one of the word processor stations.

Internet station crash.

Bathroom?

Internet station crash.

2002 Yearbook.

Yesterday's paper.

Computer crash.

"Can you tell me if someone's there? It's an emergency!"

Value Line.

Books by Jackie Collins and Alice Walker.

I explain several times the concept of attaching files to e-mail.

Thieves Paradise, by Eric Jerome Dickey.

"I'm computer illiterate." Let's leave it at that.

Passenger and immigration lists—Germans to America, 1850-1874 and 1875-1888, on CD-ROM.

W-2 form (Librarian Y tries to explain why we don't have them).

Printer advice.

In the Afternoon

Grant-proposal-writing books.

I tell a child not to run, so he skips.

Reading club.

Books in Spanish.

Angus, Thongs and Full-Frontal Snogging, by Louise Rennison (First of a series, and of course, the only one that's not on the shelf).

Both newspapers are out, sir.

Location of a halfway house, and directions, which involved several directories and guides, and the help of a nearby customer who knows the neighborhood.

Nursing careers.

Books on hold are at the circulation desk, sir.

Books on hold are at the circulation desk, ma'am.

Internet signups: 30

Friday, July 11, 2003

In the Morning

He was writing an "editorial" on women in the military. He needed books, and a word processor. He also needed help with his wheelchair and printer advice. Meanwhile the line behind him began to grumble.

Book club.

Electrical engineering books, also ceramics.

How much tax he had to withhold from his employee's checks, and boy, what an asshole.

Computer crash.

The Lake House, by James Patterson, *Eleventh Hour,* by Catherine Coulter, *The Da Vinci Code,* by Dan Brown, *Sleep No More,* by Greg Iles, and *The Second Time Around,* by Mary Higgins Clark. I suspect this lady was about to go on vacation.

A section of *Morningstar* was missing. The woman was shocked, shocked.

Printer advice.

Pencil.

Word processors are down there, ma'am.

Printer advice.

Books on how Muslims conduct business.

She wanted the Internet so she could look up words. I gave her a dictionary. She was happy.

Manufacturers for this state, then associations.

Step-Hall-Change, by Jeanne Ray.

Chemistry books.

"I'm not familiar with the Internet." Sigh.

No, we don't have DVD players for public use.

In the Afternoon

'93 Dodge Caravan repair manual.

Pencil.

We returned your ID to you, sir.

Librarian Z is regaled with a man's tale of how much Gatorade he drinks in this hot weather.

Do we deliver books to inmates?

Basic Spanish instruction tapes and books.

How to spell "Puerto Rico."

"Do you have books on U.S. history?"

CEO of American Airlines.

Today's paper.

Internet signups: 32

Thursday, July 17, 2003

In the Morning

Local free weekly paper.

The Five Love Languages, by Gary D. Chapman.

Local Habitat for Humanity contact.

Printer advice.

Nursing career books.

Phone for Rally's Burgers.

Today's paper, then yesterday's.

Change for a ten.

Map of Wisconsin.

Yesterday's paper.

Books for fathers of special-needs children, in Spanish.

A circ clerk shows me a list of garbled mathematical equations that a customer puts in the suggestion box every few days.

Don't Call Me Brother, by Austin Miles.

"Books telling you about the dangers of red meat."

In the Afternoon

BBC sound effects library CDs volumes 7 and 18.

Louis L'Amour books.

Bathroom?

"Is he too young to use the computers?" Yes.

Printer advice.

I'm told in great detail all the problems with the microfilm readers, including the fact that it's usually the other machine that gives her trouble, etc., etc.

Computer workshop info.

A scruffy customer wants a look at the penal code.

I kick two kids out of the stacks for running.

Is such and such a group meeting here tonight?

CPT guidebooks.

Beethoven's Heiligenstadt Testament. She thought it was in a book and I spent forever looking for it, as one computer crashed, then another. When they came back up I googled it and found it in ten seconds.

Internet signups: 41

Friday, July 18, 2003

In the Morning

Books by Iyanla Vanzant. "All of them."

Printer advice.

Zip code lookup.

Literacy office phone.

I call a sir a ma'am. Fortunately, he was amused.

Racial breakdown of school districts in Dallas.

Electronics test books.

He's forgotten his username and password, and he can't type. He swears he's been to the Web site before and he has important business there. Meanwhile, the line behind him gives me dirty looks.

Kate Remembered, by A. Scott Berg.

The Beginning of Wisdom, by Leon Kass.

Franco-Prussian War books.

The man who's forgotten his username certainly never had one. He sits there trying things at random and grumbling to himself. When it asked for an e-mail address he gives his name, along with "com-dot-net." I remember him as the man who once got upset because we told him it was impossible to fax his document with a photocopier.

Tuesday's paper.

Bathroom?

Yesterday's paper.

No publisher will publish his novel, which he now keeps in a green plastic case.

He wants a quick look at his family tree on the Internet. I try to warn him. . . . He announces that he intends to start with the census.

Stapler.

In the Afternoon

A guy wants to know roughly where everything is. I point out fiction, nonfiction, and magazines. He is happy.

Address to the State Department Administrative Hearings office.

Can I help you? "Nope." This is becoming a trend.

Armageddon, by Tim LaHaye and Jerry B. Jenkins, on tape. Although I fail to locate a copy she discovers that she hadn't read *The Remnant* yet. Unfortunately, we didn't have a copy of that, either.

Today's paper.

Issues of *Dragon* from many years ago. Alas . . .

Internet signups: 31

Thursday, July 24, 2003

In the Morning

Bathroom request.

Three computer crashes.

Pay phone?

Melanin: The Chemical Key to Black Greatness, by Carol Barnes, *The African Origin of Biological Psychiatry,* by Richard King, *The Science of Melanin,* by T. Owens Moore, and *African Holistic Health,* by Llaila Africa.

Computer workshop question.

Printer advice.

Two computer crashes.

Genealogy helper.

A back issue of *U.S. News & World Report.*

She tries to access the Web using Microsoft Word.

Apply for a card at the front desk, sir.

The Long Walk Home, starring Sissy Spacek and Whoopi Goldberg.

Movie star addresses.

Books by Iyanla Vanzant.

"Can I get this covered in plastic?"

Today's paper.

Stretching, by Bob Anderson.

The meeting room is downstairs, sir.

The copier is over there.

"Is the printer plugged up?"

The Watsons Go to Birmingham—1963, by Christopher Paul Curtis, *The Giver,* by Lois Lowry, *A Wrinkle in Time,* by Madeleine L'Engle, and *Island of the Blue Dolphins,* by Scott O'Dell. All for a sixty-year-old man.

Lady, stop that tuneless whistling! (I didn't really say that). Later, I saw her at a table stabbing a finger at something in the paper while hissing.

In the Afternoon

Number of days in July.

Taber's Cyclopedic Medical Dictionary.

How to recharge your debit card.

Did an exam we're going to proctor arrive?

A customer didn't have her ID and proceeded to whine at us about it.

Addicted, by Zane, and *Baby Momma Drama,* by Carl Weber.

Six Flags employment information.

W-7 form.

Don't run!

Today's paper.

Stapler.

I go to tell some small children not to run. Their parents, or whoever was in charge of them, then shouted at them to "Come here!" Then the kids were each hit—HARD. One even fell over. It was appalling. I've broken up a couple of fights at the library before, but I'd never encountered anything like this. I had no idea what to do.

The Bell Jar, by Sylvia Plath, *Their Eyes Were Watching God,* by Zora Neale Hurston, *Slaughterhouse-Five,* by Kurt Vonnegut, and *My Antonia,* by Willa Cather. The same list as yesterday. The customer said there were 25 people in her class. We're in trouble.

Ifa Divination (no author).

The card catalog's over there, ma'am.

Internet signups: I lost count.

Saturday, July 26, 2003

In the Morning

Study room?

Today's paper.

Value Line.

"Novels about George Washington." Do you mean biographies? "Yeah, biographies and bibliographies. Primary sources."

"I can't find Great Northern Iron in *Value Line.*" He needed the expanded edition.

"It's been so long since I've been in the library. Everything's changed." However, our public copiers are pretty much the same as 20 years ago.

"I'm glad to see you here because you will find me what I want."

Bureau of Citizenship and Immigration Services branch office.

When is our next book sale?

"Does your version of Word have the mail-merge wizard?"

Local sales tax.

City map.

Leap of Faith, by Queen Noor.

In the Afternoon

Book club.

Donald Goines books.

His password won't work . . . whoops, yes it does.

Books on growing orchids.

"Can I extend the time on this book?"

He wants to know how to tear a map out of a magazine.

Black, White and Angry, by Andrew Hacker. I pulled up *Two Nations: Black and White, Separate, Hostile, Unequal,* by Andrew Hacker, but she says that isn't the one. Later, we have this discussion: Ma'am the only book we own by an author named Michael Myers is about computer networking. "That could be the one." It has nothing to do with race relations. "You sure? I'd like to look at it anyway."

Printer advice.

"I need an AM radio in Milwaukee . . . news, the call letters."

"Can I take *Morningstar* home with me?" Haha no.

"*Spanish for Dummies.*" Actually, she wanted any Spanish instruction book she could find.

Printer advice.

Printer advice.

Books on real estate investing.

Books on eBay.

Printer advice.

State lottery jackpot estimation.

Books with Spanish words pronounced. Surprisingly hard to find.

We no longer take IDs for the computers, ma'am.

Internet signups: 39

Tuesday, July 29, 2003

In the Morning

Pen.

"Sign this."

Silhouette Dreamscapes series books.

A lot of local phone company phone numbers.

Today's paper hasn't arrived yet, sir.

Study room.

The Rainmaker, but which one?

Info on the National Home Oxygen Patients Association.

Pimsleur French instruction tapes, the long series. Then the customer calls me Dennis.

In the Afternoon

Librarian Y reads *The Fabulous Sex Organ Diet,* by John Van Reginald Tomlinson III.

Harry Potter and the Order of the Phoenix, by J. K. Rowling.

Books on wild bears and flowers? Oh, wild berries . . .

Librarian Y gets a customer who wants a "pleading for a wrongful death" form.

July 18 paper.

Blood Diamonds, by Greg Campbell.

Shut up! I mean, Shhh.

Copier advice (Turn the page over, sir).

Pencil.

Can I help you? "No."

Pencil.

E-mail advice.

Stapler.

Someone lost some cassettes.

Videos on the Galapagos Islands.

"What time it is?"

Info on Stephanie Mills.

"I need a newspaper for North Carolina. What kind of papers they got in North Carolina?"

"I don't have Yahoo. I'm using Microsoft Network" (Same customer).

To Kill a Mockingbird, by Harper Lee, on CD.

Definition of "Dead heads" and "Glorytits." Much laughter on the other end of the phone.

Civil war books on tape.

Internet signups: 31

Thursday, July 31, 2003

In the Morning

(I thought rather than just give the total Internet signups at the end of the entry I would show how they appear in the course of a shift:)

My god they can talk loud in circ.

Internet.

Internet.

Internet.

Internet.

"Books on musicians, rappers."

Internet.

Internet.

Internet.

He wants to log into a job site but first he needs an e-mail account blah blah.

Printer advice.

Internet.

All the good Hotmail names are taken, sir.

Definition of "aesthetic."

Internet.

Internet.

The password you chose needs to be longer, sir.

Internet.

Tissue.

Computer workshop question.

Internet.

ASVAB books.

Telephone book.

Internet.

Local map.

Internet.

Internet.

Brilliant, by Marne Kellogg, *We Can Still Be Friends,* by Kelly Cherry, and *The Dogs of Babel,* by Carolyn Parkhurst.

Internet.

Internet.

Internet.

Internet.

Internet.

Internet.

Internet.

Internet.

Computer crash.

Computer crash.

Computer crash.

Computer crash.

Computer crash.

Computer crash. At this point I realize the network is down.

Computer workshop info.

"I like biographies and autobiographies."

Internet.

Internet.

Hillary's Scheme, by Carl Limbacher.

Internet.

Internet.

People often look bewildered when I explain that I cannot sit with them and teach them how to use the computer.

Yellow pages.

Internet.

Internet.

Internet.

Book club.

Internet.

In the Afternoon

(We had help at the computer desk by now.)

The New Thought Police and *The Death of Right and Wrong,* by Tammy Bruce.

"What is the minimum wage?"

Internet.

"Can I use your catalog?"

Footloose on DVD.

Microfilm advice.

Books on the Romanovs, esp. Anastasia.

Internet.

Local senator's address.

Kids fighting in the stacks. "No, we weren't."

Internet.

Internet.

Nursing exam practice books. What a rude woman.

Librarian Y gets a request for kosher pepper books, I think.

Internet.

Internet.

Internet.

Of Mice and Men, by John Steinbeck (on tape). I couldn't find it. "That's okay, I still got the Cliffs Notes."

Chapter 3

Something Is Not Working Here

"THE COMPUTER/PRINTER/COPIER IS BROKEN"

If you read the reference diary for July 31 in the preceding section, you noticed the repeating litany of "computer crash." Now think back to those blessed days before computers entered the library. What was the worst that could happen? Well, I remember once when a clerk was filing in a card-catalog drawer. She had the rod that held the cards in the drawer pulled out to insert some new cards. She dropped the drawer on the floor and approximately 1,200 cards spilled over the rug. I know it was about 1,200 because one of the now-useless bits of trivia you used to learn in library school was how many catalog cards there were to an inch. Since card catalog drawers ran around 16" to 17", less internal hardware, 1,200 was a fairly accurate guess. That was a pretty devastating but rare event.

What other working disasters did one find in those precomputer days? Leaks in the roof? We still get these. Fights in the library? Actually, it is my impression that library users fifty years ago were better behaved. Libraries certainly were quiet! It is difficult to think of any library problem before computers that can equal the sheer staff frustration of keeping these myriad pieces of equipment functioning. How did we get in so much trouble?

Although typewriters probably were the first real technological innovation in libraries, in my opinion, the real watershed event in the transition from a quiet place to read and checkout books was the introduction of the photocopier. In 1960, the Menlo Park Library in California had a book sale, and with the proceeds purchased a photocopier, becoming one of the very first libraries to offer this service. Although the Xerox 914, which was the first automatic, plain-paper office copier, came out in 1959, it took a few years for photocopiers to become commonplace in libraries. However, certainly by the mid-1960s, library staff were having to deal with refilling paper, clearing jams, and so on, as well as fielding complaints from upset customers about copying problems. It has all been downhill from that point, with one piece of technology after another added upon the backs of library staff.

Computers, printers, copiers, plasma screens, and more provide marvelous access to information. However, with all these wonders come two immutable laws and one hypothesis.

Technology has a revenge effect.

Word processing made it possible to turn out perfect or near-perfect documents, whereas with a typewriter most people gave up after the third or fourth draft. Office productivity has not made significant improvements since the introduction of word processing. This is due at least in part to people who now repeatedly revise documents and managers who print out documents that secretaries used to handle. During the great expansion of office technology starting in the 1980s, investment in technology grew by more than 116 percent between 1980 and 1989. However, by 1985, output had increased by only 0.3 percent and by 1989 by only 2.2 percent. Some economists claim that computers and peripherals contributed no more than 0.2 percent to the growth in business productivity between 1987 and 1993. "The more powerful computing systems have become, the more human time it takes to maintain them, to develop the software, to resolve bugs and conflicts, to learn new versions, to fiddle with options" (Tenner, 1997, p. 240).

Equipment fails.

This needs no example; the daily diaries interspersed with these essays document this fact, and every library worker can attest to the reality of equipment failure.

The number of working computers in the world is fixed.

Although precise statistics are not available to confirm this hypothesis, both an empirical awareness of computer breakdown and common sense certainly give heavy weight to the belief that for every new computer manufactured, an old one breaks down. If you doubt this, just remember O'Toole's commentary on Murphy's law, which reads, "Murphy was an optimist."

Let us review these three areas briefly. Common examples of the revenge effect of technology include cases where technological improvements have made work less strenuous, leading to an increase in obesity from lack of exercise. Instead of the paperless office, our computers have led us to rely on heavier use of paper in all sorts of devices. For more examples, the reader is invited to check out *Why Things Bite Back* (Tenner, 1997).

As for the failure of equipment, people fall into two classes in the world of computers—the optimists who expect computers and peripherals to work and the pessimists who know all hardware will fail. The first class is doomed to perpetual and recurring disappointment. The second group is at least occasionally surprised. It is probably not fair to say it, but experience suggests that library administrators tend to belong to the first group, and working reference grunts belong to the second. This obviously can create a locus of discontent and stress.

Stress at the reference desk, in fact, has grown in direct correlation to the addition of each new piece of equipment. At least with photocopiers, once you filled the paper tray and cleared any existent jams, if these actions did not solve the problem, you could usually, with a clear conscience, hang an out-of-order sign on the copier and wait for the repair person. In my experience, the public was pretty understanding in those early days when it came to nonworking photocopiers—it was such a typical situation. Now, let just one public-access computer go down, or, horrors of all horrors, the network crash, and howls of anguish rise to the rafters of the library while frantic calls are made to a harassed information technology department.

An interesting additional consequence is connected with the widespread use of computers. I call this the time dilation effect. Before computers, real-time intervals, in most cases, matched a person's perception of these intervals. In other words, an objective minute took about a minute subjectively to pass—unless one were undergoing something such as dental work, in which case five minutes could stretch out indefinitely. When the first IBM 8088 PC, with a clock speed of 4.77Mhz, came out, suddenly the hours it used to take to find and retrieve information shrank to minutes. This was wonderful!

As computer speeds doubled every eighteen months (Moore's law), what took minutes to do on a computer began to take seconds. However, whenever there was a slowdown on the PC, those seconds subjectively became minutes. Then, as we entered the processor gigahertz era, with operations completed in fractions of seconds, any kind of slowdown, even of only a few seconds, now created a great sense of impatience. Even worse, this effect seems to have translated into many different aspects of life. Does anyone really believe that people were as impatient in public—grocery store lines, traffic, and so on, fifty years ago as they are now? In a very real way, I believe this is another example of the revenge effect of technology. We can do things faster than ever before, but it takes a much shorter time before our patience is exhausted.

Finally, although the hypothesis regarding the number of working computers may be a bit fanciful, here are two bits of interesting data that might make you ponder the idea: (1) "The National Safety Council (NSC) estimates that 315 million computers will be trashed in 2004, up from twenty million in 1998" (Ju, 2002) and

> (2) The Stamford, Conn.-based research firm [Gartner, Inc.] predicted that global PC shipments would reach 186.4 million units in 2004, in large part due to the estimated replacement of 100 million PCs this year. What's more, the replacement cycle is likely to continue into next year, when 120 million PCs are expected to be swapped out in favor of newer models. (Pruitt, 2004)

📖 📖 📖

A GRUNT'S DIARY: AUGUST 2003

Friday, August 1, 2003

In the Morning

U-Haul phone numbers for a number of places.

Childhood's Thief, by Rose Mary Evans.

Microfilm advice.

Don't run! (The little girl thought this highly amusing)

Book club.

Printer advice.

"Are the word processors still frozen?"

His document was in black and white and he wondered why it did not print in color.

Local freebie map.

Book club.

Map to local newspaper office.

City directories.

The Master Plan, by R. C. Allen.

The Chocolate War, by Robert Cormier.

Try not typing the URL in caps, sir.

"Indian collectables," which morphed to "collectable knives."

Nearby newspaper.

In the Afternoon

A girl calls to tell us she can't boot up her computer. I turn to Techie Y, who discovers that she has an Apex 100! Her dad had bought it at a garage sale, mistaking the 5 1/4" drive slots for CD-ROM drives.

The New York Times.

A circ clerk kicks a man off a fifteen-minutes-only Internet terminal after an hour, so he files a complaint.

Blue screen of death.

Books on optical illusions.

She broke a cassette and is all apologetic. We soothe her.

Bibles.

Don't run!

Librarian X and I have started to talk about food, which means it's late in the day.

Printer advice.

Stapler.

Who Moved My Cheese? by Spencer Johnson.

Limericks.

Weeping Willows Dance, When We Practice to Deceive, and *Promises to Keep,* by Gloria Mallette.

Somewhere near circ, a child sounds like she's being tortured.

Sorry, no Internet, we're ready to close.

Internet signups: 26

Monday, August 4, 2003

In the Morning

Don't bang on the computer keys, kid.

Here's a computer workshop schedule, ma'am.

"How long can you have a Yahoo! account until they charge you?"

Computer crash.

Computer crash.

Johnny Angel, by Danielle Steel, *Kate Remembered,* by A. Scott Berg, and *Gone Too Far,* by Suzanne Brockman.

Librarian Q gets: "I'm looking for frogs, in color."

A man lost his bike helmet. He's been in the library five minutes. . . . Whoops! He found it.

Printer advice.

Internet advice.

Study room.

Microfilm problem.

Today's paper.

"Can I burn a CD here?" Sorry.

"My computer slows down after I use it awhile . . ." Another question that should go to a tech support guy.

Basic beginner computer books.

Old dictionaries.

Printer advice.

Tecumseh motor repair manual.

"You put the copy in the machine and push the button, right?"

A woman believes our study room has whiteboards in them. White walls, yes, but not whiteboards.

Bus driving exams.

On my way to lunch a car slows down. The driver is a regular customer who wants to ask me a reference question.

In the Afternoon

"Can I use the computer?" No, you're too small. "I TOLD you," says a second kid.

ESL materials.

Stapler.

Printer advice.

Outrageous Misconduct, by Paul Brodeur.

Woman with two infant children asks Librarian Q for books on fertility.

Local Comcast phone number.

Why do people waiting at the desk assume I want to chat with them while I'm helping another customer?

Printer advice.

A man just doesn't understand why we don't permit church services in our meeting room.

Correction fluid.

Today's paper.

Test book practice guides for a test I've never heard of.

Librarian Q gets: "Do you get interpersonal library loans?" He wanted the song "Optimistic" by Sounds of Blackness.

Today's paper.

I show Mr. Interpersonal an all-music guide and he goes crazy choosing albums he wants to interpersonal loan. I am a little ashamed to say I was relieved that Librarian Q had to do the dirty work.

The August *Woman's Day* has vanished.

Investors Business Daily for last week

She wants to find a street in a nearby town, but we fail.

A customer disapproves of our stapler.

How to organize a fashion show.

Printer advice.

There's a catalog terminal here, sir.

Librarian Y kicks me off the desk.

Internet signups: 36

Thursday, August 7, 2003

In the Morning

Printer advice.

YMCA phone number.

A customer can't believe that we don't have city directories for his town and complains about our lack of service.

Bathroom.

Tape.

A man on his way to the Internet terminals mutters something about downloading a coupon for a pack of Salems.

Music Publishing, by Tim Whitsett, and *How to Make Money Scoring Soundtracks and Jingles,* by Jeffrey P. Fisher.

Fax machine?

Pencil.

In the Afternoon

"What age group is Romeo and Juliet written for?"

A lame old TV show joke comes to life: A rather obnoxious woman wants to start an etiquette school.

A lady wants to find someone in Pocono, Florida, which doesn't exist. Before I could continue with the interview, she got cut off.

A guy tries to print out a Web page only to have three different terminals crash on him.

Fax machine.

2002 issues of *Guitar Player.*

Librarian Y thinks a book cart looks "lonely."

Stapler. The customer tells me that I am a nice person.

Always True to You in My Fashion, by Valerie Wilson Wesley.

4:30 p.m., and Librarian Y and I have begun to discuss food.

Sorry ma'am, I can't go around looking for a man with a chipped tooth.

A customer knows a lot about movie history and fills Techie Y and me in on John Wayne and the Three Stooges.

Librarian Y and I have an argument about peaches and melons.

Fax machine?

Internet signups: 47

Sunday, August 10, 2003

In the Afternoon

Open on a summer Sunday. Whose idea was this?

Today's paper.

Chevrolet P-30 repair manual.

Fax machine?

Three-hole puncher?

Pen?

ILL pickups at the front desk, ma'am.

"I need books on chess . . . books on chess!" he nearly shouts.

"Methodrone maintenance."

"A book called *It* . . . is that the one with all the sexual abuse?" (Librarian R
   got this one.)

Printer advice.

The meeting room needs to be unlocked.

Damn, if MY husband talked to me like that I'd leave him.

Auto body painting.

City directories.

Pencil?

Internet access question.

A Little Inside (on DVD). .

Books are held at the front desk, sir.

City directories.

What are those kids doing under that table where all the Internet cables are?

Why is this man so surprised that we have today's paper?

Why am I here on a Sunday? Oh, to give printer advice.

More city directories.

Click on the Microsoft Word icon, ma'am.

Try turning off the caps lock, ma'am.

Don't run!

Techie X walks over. We look out the window at the sunshine and curse our
   rotten luck.

Don't run, oh, the hell with it.

Copier help (push the big green button, sir).

Fiction is over there, ma'am.

Today's paper.

I fix the copier.

Cane River, by Lalita Tademy.

Books on African-American reparations.

Techie X announces he is King of the Internet. It's time to go.

Internet signups: 8

Monday, August 11, 2003

In the Afternoon

Lüde, Crüde, and Rüde: The Story of Mötley Crüe, by Silvie Simmons.

1040-EZ forms.

I think he wants fantasy novels but he can barely speak English and he's shy.

Kleenex?

How to place a hold.

Old yearbooks.

"Should I paperclip or staple my resumé?" I suggest paper clips and he asks for five.

A basic tour of Windows '98.

Don't run!

Word advice, resumé advice, and printer advice.

He asks where the oversized books section is and I show him the large print books. Whoops.

He's got my name from my tag and he's not going to let it go.

Later he shows me an obit. "I know that guy. He's dead."

Voter registration.

Hooked on phonics.

Confessions of a Shopaholic, by Sophie Kinsella, and *Confessions of a Hollywood Columnist,* by Sheilah Graham.

The Color Purple, by Alice Walker.

1996 building code.

Don't run!

Printer advice.

Double-click, ma'am, and don't move the mouse when you do.

Librarian Z has to explain the concept of "save as" several times.

Psalms on tape.

A recent apellate decision (I find it moments after the customer had given up and left).

Obit request from Canada.

Criss-Cross (a reverse directory lookup).

Printer advice.

The Black Prince, by Iris Murdoch.

In the Evening

Herbs for Clearing the Skin, by Sarah Beckett, *Understanding an Afrocentric World View,* by Linda James Meyers, and *The Truth About AIDS,* by Ann Giudici Fettner and William A. Check.

Dolly: The Biography, by Alanna Nash.

"Any books on wrestling not the Mick Foley books?"

Scotch tape, which led to a rant about the government.

Is our color printer working?

A man donates a quarter for all the staples and tape he's used.

A couple of confusing notarizations. Some forms I don't know if I need to stamp or not . . .

A business in Mesquite, Texas.

A "chicken soup" book, but the customer doesn't know what kind of soul she has.

Astrology books.

Social statistics, or psychology statistics. She couldn't come up with better words and went off to find her syllabus.

Two more notarizations, and I'm told about her vacation worries.

Coming of Age in Mississippi, by Anne Moody, *Forged by Fire,* by Sharon Draper, and *Jubilee,* by Margaret Walker.

Lord of the Flies, by William Golding, and *Frankenstein,* by Mary Shelley.

Thursday, August 14, 2003

In the Morning

Some weather small talk.

Asbestos information, but she wants the other side of the argument.

Two notarizations.

The Secret Life of Bees, by Sue Monk Kidd.

Computer crash.

Bathroom?

Kids section?

Automotive books?

His debit card dies on him.

Local Hertz number.

Books on religion, psychology, and an author named Zeist.

The print station is having a bad morning.

Another computer crash.

Copier advice (zoom function).

Anne Rice books are over there, sir.

"A guy looked up my address online. How did he do that?"

Today's paper.

True crime books.

1983 Toyota Corolla repair manual.

The Remnant, by Tim LaHaye and Jerry B. Jenkins (on tape).

In the Afternoon

Word processor?

Librarian Y is obsessed with food these days.

Printer advice.

Tax form instructions.

Yes, sir, cassettes are listed in the catalog.

SBC toll-free number.

An abortion clinic in Houston.

The Coldest Winter Ever, by Sister Souljah.

Copier.

Librarian Y gets a customer who wants to mail order venison with food stamps.

Reports on the blackout start coming in, keeping us occupied on a slow afternoon.

Internet signups: 33

Saturday, August 16, 2003

In the Morning

Librarian X says that today we will get "intelligent, polite, good-looking customers."

Four notarizations.

Restroom?

Change?

Who provides GED study classes?

Year of Wonders, by Geraldine Brooks.

What does "AME" stand for?

Communication problems with one customer. Everything he or I or Librarian X says seems to miss the mark. A lot of confused staring.

2003 *Chase's Annual Events.*

Phone for Burlington Coat Factory.

Dictionary?

Value Line.

"I need books on the five senses," but then she starts to talk about policemen.

Another customer who tries to write a resume but has never used a word processor before, and blames it on us.

The stairway's by the front door, sir.

Our summer book club is over, ma'am.

Yes, we have old newspapers on microfilm.

In the Afternoon

How far back do our *Readers Digest*s go?

Today's paper.

Haley's Cleaning Hints, by Graham and Rosemary Haley.

A passing customer tells me I should have bought lemon Kool-Aid.

Today's paper.

Bodybuilding.

Yes, sir, we have a microfiche reader.

Fit for Life, by Harvey and Marilyn Diamond.

Today's paper.

You zoom in with this knob, sir.

Voter registration.

Sorry, we don't have a color copier, ma'am.

Today's paper.

You can get change at the front desk, ma'am.

Don't run!

Some books on Japanese candlestick stock trading, or something like that.

Daddy Cool, by Donald Goines.

"How do I read this book?"

A customer brings in a cute baby and Librarian X loses her mind.

Don't run!

Postal exam books.

Internet signups: 15

Tuesday, August 19, 2003

In the Morning

"I need to fill out this FAFSA form online I never used a computer I need help with this form, etc. . . . ." Happily, another customer takes pity and volunteers to help.

I play directory assistance for a lady.

How to set up an e-mail account. I am afraid he will be back (I was wrong).

Two notarizations.

Bathroom?

Caught looking at porn! Bad! Bad customer!

The FAFSA lady filled out the form successfully!

Naval reserve admission tests.

Kate Remembered, by A. Scott Berg, and *Living History,* by Hillary Rodham Clinton.

A lady is thrown off by HTML code in her e-mail.

"Are you going to be the one to notarize this?"

1982 BMW repair manual.

Computer workshop info.

Computer workshop info.

In the Afternoon

Printer?

It's the time of year when students flock to the library to order textbooks they're too cheap to buy.

Part of the copier falls off. Nearby, two small girls look worried.

"Claire Dux is best known for her work in what opera?"

Notarization.

They'll break a twenty at the front desk, sir.

"When do the banks close around here?"

Sorry ma'am, no scanner.

Stapler.

Traitor, by Matthew Woodring Stover.

700s?

Library card?

Michener books?

My Bloody Life, The Making of a Latin King, by Reymundo Sanchez.

Value Line.

Internet signups: 47

Monday, August 25, 2003

I come in the door, carrying my lunch even, and a customer stops me to ask a question.

In the Afternoon

"I need Alfred Hitchcock short stories."

Lies and the Lying Liars Who Tell Them: A Fair and Balanced Look at the Right, by Al Franken.

All the Ed Gorman and Walter Mosley books we have—in paperback.

BOCA codebook.

Three notarizations. I try to steal his pen.

Violets Are Blue, by James Patterson.

The Shelters of Stone by Jane M. Auel.

Kid's section is down the stairs, sir.

A customer wants Techie Y to help her, not Techie X. We talk her into it, though she keeps insisting she will miss Techie Y.

Bathroom?

Youth at Risk, ed. Dave Capuzzi and Douglas R. Gross, *Counseling Toward Solutions,* by Linda Metcalf.

The Passport Program, by Ann Vernon, and *Educational Psychology,* by Robert E. Slavin.

In the Evening

There's a scavenger hunt going on. Kids keep coming up to me and asking me strange things.

Living History, by Hillary Rodham Clinton.

Scratch paper.

Printer advice.

Philosophy, Who Needs It? by Ayn Rand.

Pencil?

Holds are at the front desk, ma'am. You're quite welcome.

A notarization not done right in the first place.

Yes, ma'am, CDs are listed in the catalog along with the books.

Early child care.

Books on Noah's Ark, "different versions." I finally realize that he wants various flood legends.

Yes, ma'am we have an online catalog right over here.

Videos on current social trends in Indian society.

Pictures of Hollis Woods, by Patricia Reilly Giff.

"The Cuba books moved!"

"Do you have any books by the author V. C. Andrews?"

He wants *Lolita,* by Vladimir Nabokov.

No, he wants it on tape.

No, he wants the movie, on DVD.

Thursday, August 28, 2003

In the Morning

A man gets offended when I suggest he can't spend all the time running his business over our Internet terminals and walks off in a huff.

A chapter of the tax code. The customer calls me a "scholar and a gentleman." Librarian Y laughs out loud.

A lady can't find the area which had the stories she wanted, but she didn't want novels, she wanted books on the South Pacific, no, books about people transferred there because other people died, of course, but it has to have a nice story.

The Fig Eater, by Jody Shields.

Computer crash.

Printer advice.

Bathroom?

Tape?

Pen?

I Capture the Castle, by Dodie Smith.

"City directory. No, this isn't the one I need."

Sorry, sir. We can't give a receipt for the copier.

Directions to the county jail.

"The microfilms are missing an issue of the paper." No, they're not.

They'll break a five at the front desk, sir.

Sorry, ma'am, we don't have a scanner.

In the Afternoon

Dictionary?

That's the address for the courthouse, sir.

Can I help you? "No."

1987 Ford Mustang repair manual.

Pot Planet, by Brian Preston.

A man seeks some statutes.

A man seeks his son. "He isn't far. I have the car keys."

Internet signups: 28

Chapter 4

The Computer Is Not Listening to Me!

COMPUTER LITERACY
VERSUS PRINTED LITERACY

A fundamental, but frequently unrecognized, difference exists between the concept of literacy as applied to using computers and literacy as it has traditionally related to the ability to read and comprehend the printed word. To understand what being computer literate means, we have to take into account several factors that simply do not exist in the world of print media.

First, using a computer successfully requires motor skills that are not required when reading a book or magazine. Leaving aside vision problems, other than physically being able to turn pages (or use some kind of adaptive technology to accomplish this), to read words on a page one does not need the kind of motor skills that a keyboard and mouse require. At first thought you may not think that being able to at least hunt-and-peck on a keyboard and move a semidetached small object by hand—and matching this to movements on a screen—is a part of literacy. However, consider that you were unable to turn the pages of a book and had no one to do this for you. Would your literate capabilities, as good as they might be, do you any good in getting at the information in that book?

Beyond this, if the best you can do is hunt-and-peck, your communication level, which is also a part of literacy, will be similar to someone with a limited understanding of English trying to understand a book. With a computer, typing skills are not enough; you also need the hand-eye-brain coordination to deal with a mouse if you are going to make effective use of the computer. For comparison, watch a small

Reference Librarianship: Notes from the Trenches
© 2006 by The Haworth Press, Inc. All rights reserved.
doi:10.1300/5672_04

child who does not understand typing or the mouse pound on a keyboard—a frustrating event familiar to all reference grunts! There is no way that the child, even though he or she may be able to understand a few letters, is able to communicate with the computer. This is a problem that elderly computer users may share, particularly when physical problems such as hand tremor exist.

Libraries may contribute to computer-use problems by a misguided attempt to "protect" other users from what an individual is seeing on a computer terminal. The recessed-monitor approach may work for a few people but creates ergonomic problems for many. It takes only a single visit to a library with many of these recessed monitors to see the problem; you have to wonder where the librarians were when the designers broached this idea. People trying to use these monitors are bent forward at awkward angles, some simply from the positioning and others because they are using bifocals. In the end, this system does not even do what it is supposed to do, since the screen can be read from side angles.

These physical limitations are trivial compared to the cognitive difference between understanding computers and the Internet versus the printed word. The best analogy to this difference comes from primitive and historical societies without a written language but with storytelling traditions. In these societies verbal text, stories, histories, and so on were fluid and changed with each telling and each generation. Even during the years when the only way that written material persisted was through monks laboring in monasteries, there was no assurance that words once written would reappear exactly the same in the next copy. These early ways of dealing with knowledge in some form that could be transmitted to others, either at the time or over generations, had more similarity to electronic text than anything that came after the invention of the printing press.

Other writers have pointed out the differences between writing in post-Gutenberg printed works and electronic writing. "Prior to the advent of electronic writing, tradition assigned to good literature the qualities of stability, monumentality, and authority" (Bolter, 1991, p. 162). Stability and authority, and above all monumentality, are not terms that one easily can associate with transient electronic writing in hyperspace. In another article, Bolter went on to point out even greater differences between electronic texts and words on paper:

Electronic hypertext is the latest in a series of technologies of writing; it is a technological innovation that is both revolutionary and evolutionary. Hypertext challenges our sense that any book is a complete, separate, and unique expression of its author. In addition to hypertextual writing, the computer also supports new forms of graphic representation and communication. As all forms of electronic communication become increasingly important in our society, we must learn how to combine these two orthogonal information spaces: the visual space of computer graphics with the semantic space of hypertext. (Bolter, 1994, p. 7)

If one accepts these distinctions, and they do seem eminently reasonable, it might help to think for a minute about the impact of these changes in the areas of perceiving and incorporating information in a usable form. Perhaps the best and clearest example to lead us into this possible morass of convoluted thinking is the blog. Although the individual diary entries in this book are quite short, anyone who has encountered some of the more complex blogs on the Internet should readily recognize the distinction between this form of writing and a typical fiction or nonfiction book.

The Internet requires a completely different way of assimilating information with all its attendant problems of authority, immediacy, impermanency, ambiguities, nonlinearity, and the sheer volume available. If librarians are to fully understand and make the most effective use of this new paradigm for the transmission of knowledge, they have to recognize and find better ways of dealing with and interpreting Web information for at least several generations to come. This will hold true until the sole users of a library are the people who are very young now and are growing up in this brave new world. At that point, who knows whether the physical library as we know it today will even exist?

Therefore, when librarians talk about computer literacy, not only do they have to consider the traditional problems of semi- and illiterate users, they also must take into account the large proportion of their user base who came to adulthood *before* the days of online catalogs and the Web. It seems overly optimistic to assume that simple, two-hour "classes" in the Internet can be sufficient to create a clientele of "literate" computer users. Most libraries probably would benefit from affiliations with such organizations as SeniorNet (www.seniornet.org), which has online computer tutorials including mouse exercises and multiple discussion groups on various computer topics. SeniorNet also can provide a curriculum for on-site instruction, including a weeks-long course on learning to handle a mouse and play cards, eight-week introductory computer classes, and word processing and spreadsheet courses. Another source that has received positive mention on PUBLIB is Generations on Line (www.generationsonline.com), which describes itself as "devoted to Internet literacy and access for the paper generation." This nonprofit organization provides online training software for seniors to libraries, senior centers, and other facilities at a price (currently $350.00 plus an annual maintenance fee).

📖   📖   📖

A GRUNT'S DIARY: SEPTEMBER 2003

Friday, September 5, 2003

In the Morning

I'm less awake than usual this morning.

"How do you get that copier started? It's got too many buttons!"

Floppies for sale at the front desk, ma'am.

2000 VW Passat repair manual.

Copier advice.

Librarian Y and I discuss strange and painful methods of execution.

Are you sure you don't have your ID with you, ma'am? (She did.)

Yesterday and Saturday's papers.

Computer crash (next time, ma'am, just press enter).

A man wants to look at sex offenders online.

Computer crash.

Computer crash.

"I'm throwing a block party, and I need limbo music."

In the Afternoon

"Music on cassettes?"

Dictionaries you can check out.

Consumer Reports.

He has a list of Caudill winners to look up.

More *Consumer Reports.* The first customer is happy to share.

Bartlett's Familiar Quotations, a "biographical reference book" (whatever that
is), and an almanac. The girl is learning how to do research on a beautiful
Friday afternoon. I don't know if I approve or not.

Praise for Librarian X. This afternoon she came out to help a guy who doesn't
speak English and had a legal problem. It took a half hour, and she talked
with him and made calls on his behalf to places. I don't know what his
problem was, but he was obviously told by government offices who don't
care to "go to the library" because we would have the answers, or the
forms. We don't. Librarian X was the only person who cared, took the
time, and (Yesss!) phoned and reprimanded the assholes in the offices who
had blown off the customer. Librarian X Rocks!

Sorry, ma'am. We don't tutor kids.

I find the consumer info the second lady wanted (replacement windows) online. She thanks me by urging me to see *The Lion King.*

Don't run!

Printer advice.

I'm starving.

Techie X announces again that he is "King of the Internet," but he always
says this when it's quiet.

Internet signups: 21

Tuesday, September 9, 2003

In the Morning

Old newspapers on microfilm.

Someone please shut those kids up. . . .

Try the printer over there, sir.

More microfilm issues.

A police detective wants to look at our Internet logs.

"How do I get free Internet at home?" This leads to a long discussion about ISPs, speeds, and online games.

At this rate I many have to go over and load every single microfilm reel he wants . . .

The microfiche reader is being used, sir.

Printer advice.

Don't hang from the counter, kid.

"History of Europe, 1715 up to now?"

Printer advice.

I suggest to a woman that she save her word processor document. She just stares blankly at me.

The Maintenance Man, by Michael Baisden.

Pen.

Bathroom.

Books on the history of Protestantism.

Barron's.

Don't run!

"Your library's Internet service: is it a dial-up?"

"Do I insert the card like this?" Just try it, lady.

More printer advice.

Algebra books.

Israel in Egypt, and *Judas Maccabaeus,* by Georg Friedrich Händel.

My computer crashes.

Lottery Master Guide, by Gail Howard.

In the Afternoon

Real estate contract forms.

All the online catalogs are the same, ma'am.

Stephen Covey books, but I think it's too late for this lady.

"About a year ago I checked out a book about hip-hop . . ."

Printer advice, but he gets bored and wanders off. He comes back.

Duties of local aldermen.

Teacher certification study guides.

Religious attitudes toward cremation, especially the Baptists.

Today's paper.

A brother-in-law's phone number.

Today's paper.

Pen.

An atlas he can check out.

Today's paper.

I don't know if the Web site will charge you or not, ma'am, if you don't tell me what it is (I phrased it a little differently).

Pen.

Pen.

Someone's phone number.

My computer crashes.

Today's paper.

Scorpions.

Heart disease.

Lecture.

Front desk will sell you a disk, sir.

Word processors over there, ma'am.

How to renew books over the phone.

The spelling of "rotten."

Pencil.

Newspapers for August.

She asks where the LC cataloged books are. I point out that we use Dewey here. She deduces from this that we do not have any books on child labor law.

Internet signups: 57

Wednesday, September 10, 2003

In the Morning

Invasion of Privacy, by Perri O'Shaughnessy.

The Journals of Sylvia Plath.

Atlas of the North American Indian, by Carl Waldman.

Sorry, no obit requests over the phone, sir.

Still no dictionaries to check out.

Harry Potter and the Order of the Phoenix, by J. K. Rowling, on CD.

Reservation Blues, by Sherman Alexie, and *The Bluest Eye,* by Toni Morrison.

Old city directories.

Apparently he didn't want to wait over the phone.

She wants to e-mail her boyfriend nude pics of herself. I show her how to attach files.

Try an online catalog, ma'am.

Pencil.

Constitution guide, in Spanish.

How to Be Your Dog's Best Friend, by the Monks of New Skete.

Computer crash.

Printer advice.

Counseling (vocational guidance).

More e-mail attachment questions.

Stapler.

"I need world history. I couldn't find it on the computers."

Printer advice.

Friday's paper.

Try the kid's section, kid.

More e-mail attachment questions.

No, you can't check out that GED book, ma'am.

Chupacaba or *The Goat Sucker.*

Two nearby library phone numbers.

"Do you proctor exams?"

Constitution guide, in English this time.

Bathroom.

Internet signups: 68

Thursday, September 11, 2003

In the Morning

You can recharge your debit card over there, sir.

Neither Librarian X or Y are wearing their little flag pins. Terrorists.

Allister 710 garage door opener repair.

A disk caught in the A: drive. Techie Y saves the day.

Printer advice.

Computer crash.

Another customer wants to know which ISP to join.

Sorry, ma'am, we don't have PowerPoint for XP on our machines.

Free Help from Uncle Sam, by William M. Alarid.

"I'm used to the old card catalogs." Why do people keep saying that? We haven't had a card catalog around here for fifteen years.

A customer takes one look at me and turns to Librarian Y for help. . . .

ASVAB book.

Thanks, sir, but you don't need to sign out.

In the Afternoon

Bathroom.

The Vibe History of Hip-Hop

Auto repair manuals in Spanish.

Printer advice.

A Plato dialogue, but his syllabus doesn't say which one.

Microfilm reader advice.

You can change your address at the front desk, ma'am.

"I need information on Abraham Lincoln and Andrew Jackson."

Computer crash.

Today's paper.

Books by Eric Jerome Dickey.

Don't run!

Phone to a nearby church that doesn't exist.

Pen.

Her daughter loaded a program on her home computer that won't allow a user to boot up without a password. Guess what they've forgotten . . .

Internet signups: 24

Tuesday, September 16, 2003

In the Afternoon

Books to identify trees.

Printer advice.

A big list of literary styles and movements which she needs defined.

Cahokia civilization.

Oprah books, but not *East of Eden.* She wants "newer, up-to-date" books.

You can get a library card at the front desk, sir.

Cartooning books.

"Art books." She refuses to narrow it down.

The copier is over there, ma'am.

An atlas to check out.

Mexican independence.

The spelling of "Milwaukee."

"I need a newspaper. . . . Any one." Actually she was looking for articles on "street racing."

In the Evening

I fax a computer workshop schedule.

"The index number for asbestos?"

Phone for a Fort Lauderdale newspaper.

Some Things I Never Thought I'd Do, by Pearl Cleage.

The Coldest Winter Ever, by Sister Souljah.

"Can I use your phone?"

Bible study books.

"Books on Mexican independence?" We're beginning to run low.

Biographies are over there, ma'am.

Copier advice.

I knew I should have walked her over to the biographies. . . .

Yes, you can use a study room, if your little group shuts up (I didn't put it quite that way).

Copier advice.

"Nice day today." I wouldn't know.

Sweep: Awakening, by Cate Tiernan.

"What time is it?"

Our security guy strolls by. "Even the kids are bringing babies in tonight."

You can recharge your debit card over there, sir.

Stapler.

Books on hair styling.

A woman got a free computer and wants to wipe out everything and start fresh with Win98. Techie X and I bewilder her with advice for 30 minutes.

Disappearing Acts, by Terry McMillan.

Internet signups: 14

Thursday, September 18, 2003

In the Morning

Newspapers and city directories from 1935.

The Middle Pillar, by Israel Regardie, *Simplified Qabala Magic,* by Ted Andrews, and *Astral Projection Plain & Simple,* by Osborne Phillips.

Nursing exam books.

Yesterday's paper.

Librarian Y gets a gentleman with an "e-mail situation." He wants to sign up for Hotmail because he hasn't found any "soulmates" through Yahoo! Mail. I've noticed that the female librarians usually wind up with these sorts of questions.

Patrons who ask for city directories always want more city directories.

Computer crash.

Consumer info on digital cameras.

Sunday's paper, sports section.

Copier's over there, ma'am.

Stapler.

Today's paper.

TangognaT has caught the disease. Sorry, TangognaT. (TangognaT had decided to try a few "Ref Grunt" style posts on her blog.)

Colorado travel books.

Missing reading glasses are still missing.

In the Afternoon

La Maestria del Amor, by don Miguel Ruiz.

Today's paper.

Printer advice.

"Is Librarian Q there?"

More printer advice.

Today's paper.

A local university course catalog, and books on "management confrontation."

The Da Vinci Code, by Dan Brown.

Books on copyrights.

True crime books.

Books by Louise Rennison.

An Anthropologist on Mars, by Oliver W. Sacks.

Sorry, sir, our next book sale isn't for a couple months.

Internet signups: 27

Tuesday, September 23, 2003

In the Morning

Our public terminals are down today for a network upgrade.

Gee, it's so quiet . . .

Madame Secretary, by Madeleine Albright.

Love poetry.

"What day will the computers be available?"

My boss steals the only pen at the desk.

The copier will make change for you, ma'am. She later hands me a forgotten social security card. "This was superimposed on my copy." She is peeved.

County courthouse—adoption records.

Department of Children and Family Services, but she hangs up before I can get the number.

"I want to open a business in this town and I need to know all about it."

"What time do we get computers?"

Dictionary.

A customer walks over to one of the blank computer screens and looks at it sadly.

Local chamber of commerce.

Price guide for old bottles.

"Can I use an Internet terminal?" Sorry.

"Not at all today?" Not at all today.

"Net's down today?" Yep.

Pencil.

"Internet, please." Sorry.

Two more customers smile and hold out their IDs . . . I shake my head.

Local Chevrolet dealership.

"Excuse me, I need to print out a resumé." Sigh.

A customer wants to know the status of two holds.

"Is there anywhere else around here that would have a computer?"

"The computers are down?" Yes. "Holy shit."

Which R. A. Salvatore book or series to read next. . . ?

"Books on industrial electricity."

Another would-be Net surfer gives me a sad smile and wanders away. . . .

Bathroom.

The Da Vinci Code, by Dan Brown.

In the Afternoon

One customer gasps when I tell her the news.

The next one looks disgusted and says "Awww!"

Others just look disgusted.

"Aw, damn."

Librarian Y and I discuss how aching toes predict things.

"No wonder nobody's here!"

Another customer settles for old yearbooks.

Our Spanish-speaking librarians are unavailable, but it's hard to explain that to the customers. Librarian Y enlists a nearby customer to help.

"San Diego newspapers?"

Dictionary to check out.

"Books on drawing graffiti?" Sorry. "How about cars?"

Some customers demand to know why, as if it is a conspiracy.

Today's paper.

One customer sees the empty computers and freezes, arms rigid at his sides, staring, mouth open.

The paper clip shortage continues, so I give her binder clips.

Some of our customers grimace.

Sorry, sir. Not today.

"Do those computers work?" Not today.

"Damn, that's right. I forgot."

"Do you have the algebra II textbooks from school?"

Computer workshop information.

Today's paper.

Math books.

A small of wave of Latino authors kids need to look up.

Sorry, you can't check out cameras here.

The Purpose-Driven Life, by Rick Warren.

My Bloody Life, by Reymundo Sanchez.

Another kid with another name. It would help if he had the name right, or the country the man was from.

"I need an experiment by August Weisman." What field was he in? "Evolution. He did an experiment about Lamarck."

The Origin of Humankind, by Richard Leakey. She had found it on the shelf, but she was too short to reach it.

"Child support books. Legal stuff."

Sorry.

Sorry.

Number of times I broke a Web surfer's heart: Please add up the ones listed here and add about twenty, if you care to know.

Friday, September 26, 2003

In the Morning

Yellow pages for a state.

A customer is starting a genealogy project.

Algebra books.

We're still having an occasional network problem.

1960-1961 city directories and yearbooks.

No ID? No Internet.

Naked Empire, by Terry Goodkind.

Computer crash.

Nearby zip code.

Books by J. California Cooper.

I gave her the wrong zip code!

Server reboot, and I'm turning customers away again.

Culture and Psychology, by David Matsumoto.

Computer freeze-up.

Sorry, sir, no headphones for computers.

Newspaper back issues.

God Is Up to Something Great, by Tony Evans.

More rebooting.

Part of the network works, part doesn't.

Copier advice (turn the paper sideways, ma'am).

Guys, keep it down, please.

"Do you work here? I need two copies of these."

Alcohol and drug abuse books.

Cost per ounce of platinum in 1979.

In the Afternoon

Why is our Internet guy giving a customer grammar advice?

Don't run!

Sorry, we don't have your sunglasses at this desk, ma'am.

ILL follow-up.

Don't run!

We don't have your sunglasses, I promise you.

And Then There Were None, by Agatha Christie.

Daughters of the Dust on DVD.

Techie Y stops by to mutter something in the tongue of his people. He vanishes and the server goes down.

Today's paper.

Last Sunday's paper.

Copier advice (turn the paper sideways, sir, no, not that way . . . no . . . that way . . . no, the way you had it before . . .).

We have more online catalogs over there, ma'am.

You have to be high school age to use the computers . . . and don't run!

September 5 paper.

"How many CDs can you check out at one time?" This is an English class assignment.

The Piano Tuner, by Daniel Mason.

Oops, we actually do have those sunglasses.

Books on becoming an electrician.

Out of the stacks, kids.

A biography of Thomas Hobbes, also *Leviathan,* which was surprisingly hard to find in paper form. . . .

Librarian Y wants to know if it is raining. I suggest she look out the window. She says she is afraid to.

Magic tricks.

Kelley Blue Book Web address.

The Coldest Winter Ever, by Sister Souljah.

Internet signups: 34

Monday, September 29, 2003

In the Afternoon

Printer advice.

Tape.

"Oh, geez, I dialed the wrong number, sorry."

Our city population, the library's total square feet, and number of items we own. Surprisingly hard to find.

A customer picks up his lost ID.

Harry Potter and the Sorcerer's Stone, by J. K. Rowling (tape).

Poetry. No particular poet, poem, time period, country, whatever. Just poetry.

Kill and Tell, by Linda Howard.

Printer advice.

Phone book for a nearby community.

Local manufacturing and services directories.

Local map.

Printer advice.

Change at the front desk, sir.

In the Evening

Pencil.

Program.

That's not the printer, ma'am.

"Can anybody help me with this machine over here?"

Pencil.

Pen.

Books of "fabrics." "Like how cotton and wool are made." Actually, she wanted books on textile manufacturing.

"Can we use any library card here?"

"Computers, right?"

The Infinite Plan, by Isabel Allende.

That's not an online form, sir. You have to print it out.

Out of the stacks, kids. Stop hitting him with that book.

Books about Marie Louise Élisabeth Vigée-Lebrun.

A child uses an online catalog to play Rachmaninoff.

Address to a circuit court.

Our easy-reading books for adults are no longer there. It's just empty shelf. Both the customers and I are mystified.

Don't run! The kid didn't even look up.

Outside, the car fire has been doused.

A customer tells everyone within earshot how long it took to print his document.

Program.

I reset an online catalog.

Keep it down, please.

Dictionaries to take home. Dang, we're out again.

Biographies. All of them.

"Do you have *Consumer's Buying Guide?*" Which one?

Yay, the little middle-schooler found the book herself!

A man walks out of his way to thank me. I didn't even help him.

Stapler.

Don't run!

Printer advice.

Internet signups: 12

Days until my vacation: 4

Tuesday, September 30, 2003

In the Morning

"I need endangered birds, the laws, federal, state, city, for pigeons."

Human sexuality books for a child development project.

City directories.

I hope you saved your document, ma'am, because we have to reboot.

A nice old lady donates all of her Danielle Steel books to the library.

ESL classes in the area.

ESL classes in the area.

Her floppy crashes each one of our WPs.

August newspapers.

"Where's the printer?"

Weekend classifieds.

A customer manages to fill out the Yahoo! Mail account form (to my surprise) but then realizes that she can't send her sheets of paper this way.

When a customer asks for a week's worth of newspapers, bring the following week as well.

"Can I post this?" I suppose.

Street maps.

ASVAB books.

Local map.

Books on Microsoft Access.

Massage therapy.

Dictionary.

In the Afternoon

The House on the Lagoon, by Rosario Ferre.

We don't have your ID, sir.

There's no one in the state that I can find with that name, ma'am. Or that name either.

Copies of *Poet's Market,* and others to check out.

"Are these all the computers that's in here?"

Paper jam in the microfilm copier.

Sunday's paper.

"Arqroar" = *Art of War.* The customer stares at the cover. "This isn't by Machiavelli."

How to break into commercials.

"Do you have Yahoo I can download?"

Dictionary.

Uncle Tom's Cabin, by "Harriet Beechum."

WPs are over there, sir.

"Where can I get a membership card?"

Yesterday's and today's paper, also a name lookup in Michigan.

Last Wednesday's paper.

She wants "West Side stories," but not the musical. In the end she doesn't have enough additional info to help me out.

Dog training books.

"The book was here yesterday."

Tissue.

Today's paper is out. So is yesterday's.

Librarian Y gets: "Is 'Sunshine on my shoulders' based on a book?"

September newspapers.

Out of the stacks, kid.

We don't have nearly enough books about winemaking, but maybe we shouldn't encourage anyone.

Octavio Paz.

He is going through every shelf, examining every book with a black spine.

Techie X reports that one by one the public terminals are locking up. It's like watching the spread of a virus.

A customer calls and asks if the computers are working. He must have had a premonition.

I point out and demonstrate a great number of research sources for a woman I find attractive.

JC Penney phone number.

"You just call me a bitch?" No one knows what he is talking about.

There are four teenage kids at the copier and they can't figure out which way to turn the paper.

I refill the microfilm printer.

Internet signups: 49

Days until my vacation: 3

Chapter 5

The Library Does Not Have
What I Want

REPRISE AND CODA

In an earlier section we discussed the library as Alice's Restaurant, where "you can get anything you want." Why, then, "Reprise and Coda?" Why revisit this subject? I am taking the word *reprise* not in its preferred musical connotation, but rather in a secondary sense of a repetition. Similarly, I mean *coda* not as a musical piece, but as "an additional section at the end of a text, for example, a literary work or speech, that is not necessary to its structure but gives additional information" (Microsoft Encarta, 2004). In other words, there is more to be said on this topic!

Given the plethora of resources now available in many libraries, as so well exemplified by the each month's diary in this book, why do staff still hear the refrain, "How come the library doesn't . . . ?" "Why don't you offer word processing on your public computers?" (Answer: Some libraries do—and what does this have to do with the public library mission?) "Why can't I get my e-mail on your computer?" (Answer: In many libraries you can—when did this become part of the public library mission?)

In the late 1980s, Patrick Williams wrote an extremely perceptive book titled *The American Public Library and the Problem of Purpose* (Williams, 1988). Unfortunately, given the way that many public libraries have developed, I suspect that the people—library administrators on their way up—who could have benefited most from Williams's insights never read the book.

Among other salient facts, Williams describes a speech by Lowell Martin (the 1982 Bowker Memorial Lecture) in which Martin said li-

doi:10.1300/5672_05

braries suffered from trying to do too much, that the library had tried to be, "the people's university, the student's auxiliary, the children's door to reading, the free bookstore, the information agency, the scholar's workshop and the community center." However, there was a "fatal gap between claims and accomplishments, between expectations and reality, between aspiration and resources" (Williams, 1988, p. 130).

Not only have some libraries tried to be all of these things, but in the late 1970s (and persisting in a number of places today) there existed the idea of the library as "marketer." Some "with-it" libraries now refer to marketing efforts as following the "retail model." (I will come back to this in Chapter 9 when I talk about the Barnes & Noble/Starbucks approach to public library services.)

Finally, Williams described a dark side to the then-prevalent emphasis on the collection of statistics (exemplified by *Output Measures for Public Libraries*). He wrote, "librarians have never given enough attention to the possibility that statistics may be used primarily to advance the private and personal purposes of librarians" (Williams, 1988, p. 128). That is, by focusing on increasing statistics of circulation, program registration, and so on, the unacknowledged reason may be to advance the library director's career and reputation as well as to increase income. This may sound harsh and cynical, but I suspect that some working staff may hear at least a faint ring of truth in the suggestion.

If some major library voices saw these kinds of problems in the 1980s, what about now, when libraries offer many new services, most somehow tied to electronic resources? Some of our public libraries, in addition to the roles mentioned in Martin's speech, also try to be a competitor to Internet cafés, offering not only snacks but wireless access to the Internet, an entertainment forum through plasma screen displays, an after-school day care center, a daytime homeless shelter, an IRS tax form distribution center, and more things limited only by the administration's capacity to dream and sometimes by cost.

Leaving aside the additional staff stressors, how can our public keep demanding more? The answer lies in understanding the difference between a public good and a private good. A public good is something that no one would produce for individual profit. Two properties must exist to qualify something as a public good. One is that an individual who receives a benefit from a public good does not diminish benefits to other individuals. Although you might argue that if one person has a book checked out or is using a public workstation, someone else cannot access the same resource. Since a library has multiple resources (books, etc.) and time limits on their use, this argument would fail. The second property of a public good is that once it is created, it is impossible to prevent people from gaining access to the good. For most of the history of the public library movement in the United States, libraries have qualified as a public good.

Granted, sometimes libraries do take actions that seem to be contrary to this second property. However, in the larger sense, public libraries still believe they should be free and open to all—even if they have to charge for some basics, such as printing from PCs.

A private good is typically a market good transferred from a seller to a buyer in exchange for money. Once someone purchases and consumes a private good, for example a piece of pie, no one else can use that same exact good.

As libraries buy into the retail concept, adding more and more services, redesigning workspaces to resemble bookstores and cafés, putting in expensive plasma screen displays for entertainment, the public quite naturally begins to think of more things that this institution could offer. This is a basic factor in the marketing of private goods. You increase expectations in order to increase your sales. In fact, I suspect the public would not even use the term "institution" to describe a public library anymore. The library has public computers and a coffee shop? Starbucks provides wireless (Wi-Fi) access for customers with laptops, why doesn't the library do the same? If the library is rich enough, it probably will. Then, residents of nearby condominiums realize that they can actually piggyback on the Wi-Fi network from the library. The network is briefly down and complaints start coming in to the library. "If you're going to provide this service, it should work!" Eventually, the library may have to go out for a bond issue to build a more modern library with more powerful wireless networks.

Meanwhile, in trying to do everything for everyone, it seems inevitable that at some point the whole house of cards may collapse, possibly in an economic downturn where the tax base erodes. If that point arrives, and libraries have discarded books to make room for electronic access and reduced staffing for reference services, what happens then to this venerable institution?

One other factor in this race to have the latest technological innovation in libraries that believe they can afford to do this is the economic disparity that exists between the haves and have-nots as regards access to public library services. The United States has more than 15,000 public libraries. Not all of these belong to multilibrary systems with a large tax base. Many are small and poorly funded, with perhaps only one staff member with a graduate degree. Hours of service may be extremely limited. Why, when freedom of information is such an important element of a free and democratic society, should that access be dependent upon the accident of where one happens to live? Is the greater good—that is, the right of the people to information—best served by some libraries being able to afford the very latest toys, whether or not they really advance the primary library mission, while others cannot even afford to hire an MSL graduate as a director? Is this an argument for a form of socialized library service? Perhaps. However, since the United States cannot even seem to deal with equitable health care for all, the idea of equitable library service for all probably is nothing but a pipe dream.

📖 📖 📖

A GRUNT'S DIARY: OCTOBER 2003

Wednesday, October 1, 2003

In the Morning

Some Harry Potter tapes.

I show her the Yahoo! Mail page.

I reset the printer.

Techie Y comes up and tears my computer to pieces. Unfortunately he puts it back together again.

"Is Librarian X there?"

Computer crash.

Phone book.

The machine hates his debit card.

Program.

The Swimming Dragon, by T. K. Shih.

The machine hates another debit card.

Printer advice.

Answer your damn cell phone. . . .

Computer crash.

Language barrier.

Copier advice.

Value Line.

The Secret Language of Birthdays.

The Mark of the Angel, by Nancy Huston; and *The Growing Seasons,* by Samuel Lynn Hynes.

In the Afternoon

Computer crash.

Antique prices.

Yellow pages.

Che Guevara.

Bruce Lee.

I leave the desk early to do some real-life things.

Internet signups: 46

Days until vacation: 2

Thursday, October 2, 2003

In the Morning

A customer can't get rid of the porn sites the previous customer was viewing.

Computer crash.

Try a machine that's turned on, sir.

"I need a couple copies made. Do I just put in the money and do it?"

I throw away a scrap of paper that a customer had scrawled an important phone number on.

Yes, sir, the copier will reduce.

I demonstrate the microfilm reader.

Printer advice.

There's a pay phone in the lobby, sir.

Gardening books, my first reference question of the day.

Notarization.

Computer crash.

Computer crash.

Guitar tabs for *Sleepwalk,* by Larry Carlton.

Microfilm reader demonstration.

Perpetual calendar.

A lousy stinking salesman.

In the Afternoon

"I need one of you Internet geniuses." Then go over there, sir.

"Is Librarian X there?"

Librarian Y and I discuss garlic, green onions, and ginger.

English language instruction tapes.

2004 ASVAB book.

A book by Bernard Natheson, which I could not find.

Notarization.

Librarian Y got all the hard questions today.

Internet signups: 29

Days until vacation: 1

Monday, October 20, 2003

In the Afternoon

The public Internet stations are down. It's scheduled maintenance to fix the last scheduled maintenance.

He points to the empty terminals. "What time?" Not today. "What time tomorrow?"

He wants to ILL schoolbooks for the entire semester.

Not today, sir. They're down.

They're down.

Yes, all of them.

Yes, that one, too.

Sorry, they're down. "Even e-mail?"

Librarian X isn't here, ma'am.

Actually, most of the customers are taking it pretty well.

Lonely Planet guides for Jamaica, Costa Rica, and Barbados.

"Not at all?" Not at all.

Voter registration.

"Books on teeth."

A couple of textbooks. They never learn.

I promise you, ma'am, that we've never had Texas newspapers. "Oh, maybe it was phone books."

Sorry, they're down today.

A customer asks who is responsible. I point to Techie Y and the Consultant and say to blame them. Techie Y points to the Consultant and backs away.

Citizenship exam books.

Articles on teacher certification. I have to bring out the old Readers Guide.

In the Evening

Yes, you could sit at the Internet terminal with your mom, but we're not up today.

Sorry, ma'am, I haven't seen your sister in a white turtleneck.

Sorry, the computers are down. Maybe tomorrow, too.

They're fixing something.

That's right, they're down all over the library.

Sorry.

Today and probably tomorrow, too. "Wow. . . ."

Books on coaching fifth-grade basketball.

Contact information for an event we held Friday.

Sorry, they're down.

You can't use that disk here today, sir. I don't care if there is a slot for it.

Pencil.

Books on a specific type of bat: The "big-eared bat."

"The absolute location" of this town. I get him the latitude and longitude. "Is that absolute?"

They're down.

Red-tailed monkeys. "That's what our teacher called them. He's usually wrong."

Sorry, they're down.

"Location of this town, in the air." I assume he means aerial photos.

Don't run!

Blank paper.

"Witchcraft books, or something like that."

Drivers education books, followed by cookbooks and aerobics tapes.

Married but Still Looking, by Travis Hunter.

Books by Luis Rodriguez.

Local police chief's bio, then the mayor, then entertainers and sports figures.

The Richest Man in Babylon, by George Clason, on tape.

Mandrills.

Computer workshop information, financial counseling, and local job openings.

Sorry, we don't have a color printer right now.

Videos are down the stairs, sir.

Today's paper.

Sorry, they're down.

The weekend paper.

There's another copier downstairs.

There's plenty of paper in the copier, ma'am. It just needs more money.

Sorry, sir, they're down today.

Why yes, little girl, you can copy pages from the encyclopedia.

"Who did that watercolor on the wall?"

Fiction books are over there, sir.

Copier advice.

Don't run! Christ, they're adults.

Internet heartbreaks: I count 21, but there were more.

Tuesday, October 21, 2003

In the Morning

Local driver's license phone.

"I need to make a copy but I need it to go sideways."

Tax form 55-something or other.

Copier advice they didn't need.

Copier advice.

Paying for college without going broke.

The printer isn't jammed, sir, it needs more money (I had a similar question yesterday. These things come in waves).

Yearbooks, 1932-1934.

"Basic reading books."

Human cell disorders.

That's an online catalog, sir, not an Internet terminal.

Scrap paper and dictionary.

Printer advice.

Yes, ma'am, there is indeed a book waiting for you to pick up.

You can buy a disk at the front desk, ma'am.

In the Afternoon

1996 Chevy Van repair manual.

Local Habitat for Humanity phone.

Stapler.

Today's paper.

He needs it again.

1040EZ for 2002 and 2003.

Yes, sir, there's a book waiting for you at circ. No, I can't tell you the title over the phone.

"Books on bartending drinks. Up to date."

City directory.

He looked like he had a question, but in fact he was just looking at me strangely.

Another city directory.

I guess he thinks it acceptable if he takes his cell phone into the stacks. No one goes in there.

"The old GED book."

Printer advice.

Put the camera away, sir.

"Books with all the tobacco lawsuits. I'm doing a paper." Also an MLA handbook.

El Salvador.

Phone book.

"Where are these books at?" That call number's for a CD, ma'am.

"Books on witchcraft, and dead people." Make up your mind.

Mummies.

Intermediate algebra.

More El Salvador.

Still more El Salvador.

Yesterday's paper.

I can't figure out if geography has changed as a science since I went to school, or if these students are confused.

Sorry, you're too young to use the computers up here. I don't care what the kids' librarian said.

A man who can no longer walk well asks for books on running.

The origin of the jack-in-the-box.

"Is this picture more cultural or physical?" It's the geography student again.

Internet signups: 29

Wednesday, October 22, 2003

In the Morning

Yes, you can sign up for an Internet terminal again, sir.

Please please please get that screaming infant out of here.

You need an e-mail account to send e-mail, sir.

I don't know your password, sir.

Printer advice.

They'll break a five at the front desk, ma'am.

She saw it on TV: a police chief murders his wife. She has forgotten the name of the police chief, the show, and what channel it was on.

Try the copier over here . . . oh, sorry, no color copies.

I think she found her man: *Murderer with a Badge,* by Edward Humes.

What Becomes of the Brokenhearted? by E. Lynn Harris.

Printer advice.

Yahoo! keeps rejecting his user name. "I tried everything."

Did Erik Larson ever go to UIUC?

A long line of people seeking printer advice and muttering to themselves.

Investor's Business Daily.

Internet signups: 16

Thursday, October 23, 2003

In the Morning

Print server reboot.

Terminal reboot.

They'll give you a card at the front desk, ma'am.

City directory.

The Power of a Praying Parent, by Stormie Omartian.

"Why do you sign up people for the Internet?"

Sorry, we have no artwork to loan out.

Vincent Van Gogh. "This one." He shoves a photo in my face.

Printer advice, and a ton of hand-holding.

You can sit down at any machine you want, ma'am.

More hand-holding for the same customer.

Resumé books.

The Watsons Go to Birmingham—1963, by Christopher Paul Curtis.

Sorry, sir, your ILL hasn't arrived yet.

All his money is in his wallet, which is in his car, which is miles away. How did he even get here?

Terminal reset.

Printer advice.

Chemistry books in Spanish.

A book of Polish cooking he had looked at yesterday.

Conan books.

Terminal reset.

Don't call me buddy.

Terminal reset.

Title 7 stuff online.

It's nothing you did, sir. It's the stupid computer.

Terminal reset.

In the Afternoon

Over the River and Through the Woods, by Joe DiPietro, and the score for *The Pirates of Penzance.*

Copier advice.

Resume books.

Sorry, ma'am, no one turned in your ID.

Today's paper.

Printer advice ("I sent it to the server and only one page came up so it was weird").

"Internet Explorer and the other eight elements."

Patents.

Printer advice. They get mad because they have to pay.

Careers in occupational therapy.

Three different workstations refuse to print his document.

Some 11-year-olds want to read *Lowrider* magazine.

Definition of the word Watusi.

GED book.

Often when I ask a kid not to hang from the counter, his or her parent gets upset with the kid. Why? If I was that age I'd hang from the counter, too. That's what counters are for.

Occupational Outlook Handbook.

She's going back to college and needs forms, catalogs, etc.

Roses.

Perfumes.

The battle of Little Bighorn.

Books on stepfamilies, in Spanish.

Copier advice (Turn the book sideways, sir).

The copier needs toner.

Internet signups: 48

Saturday, October 25, 2003

In the Morning

How to back up a floppy.

Local college catalog.

Disks at the front desk, ma'am. "Are they already programmed?"

A customer suggests that we hire him. Fortunately, he is kidding.

Yahoo! Mail hates his account, but likes mine.

He needs an outlet for his laptop.

Printer advice.

Moon on the Water, by Mort Castle, and *Black Butterflies,* by John Shirley.

"Is the meeting room open December 7th?"

"The computer ain't acting right."

Librarian Y gets a customer who wants "the history of dreams."

America's Real War, by Daniel Lapin, *Stories and Poems for Extremely Intelligent Children of All Ages,* ed. Harold Bloom, and *30-Minute Meals,* by Rachael Ray.

Yahoo! Mail hates three more customers.

"You see anyone with a baby?"

The kids' section is downstairs, ma'am. Coincidently, so are the videos.

"Books by these authors." The sheet lists twenty names.

Books on geishas.

Juventud en Extasis, by Carlos Cuauhtemoc Sanchez.

Books on body language.

Nearby libraries.

In the Afternoon

Led Zeppelin biographies.

My computer crashes.

A customer reports that the ads are missing from today's paper.

I want to put up a sign that says "Go Away." Librarian Y thinks I shouldn't.

Book sale information.

The print server decides to print without charging a customer, who is pleased.

Today's paper.

I suppose there are worse phone ringer tunes than "The Old Folks at Home."

I leave the desk early.

Internet signups: 59

Sunday, October 26, 2003

In the Afternoon

Scarlet Empress, starring Marlene Dietrich.

True crime books.

"Books about Jah-Wars." Come again? "The cat: Jah-War."

There are more online catalogs over there, ma'am.

There's scrap paper in that box, sir.

Marketing books.

Local plasma center phone.

Flamenco dancing.

No photo ID? Sorry, no Internet.

No photo ID? Sorry, no Internet. "That . . . sucks! This library is mutter mutter," as he walks away.

Rodney King.

The copier is right over there, sir.

A *Barron's* from September.

Scissors.

Our elderly customers are often the loudest.

Librarian W gets a customer doing a report on behavioral psychology for his world history class. . . . That's what he says. Whenever Librarian W asks him a question it takes him about five seconds to answer.

Dictionary.

The brain-dead customer comes back. "I found the Web site for it." We give him our blessings.

Shut up already!

Local map.

Print server reboot.

1986 BMW 325 repair manual.

She needs a historical novel. Any one.

Sorry we don't have an index to the local paper.

Antiabortion videos.

Press "Legal" before pressing "Print," ma'am.

Today's paper.

The Great Unravelling, by Paul Krugman, and *Master of the Senate,* by Robert Caro.

He lost his insulated coffee cup.

Don't run!

English-Spanish dictionaries.

Can I help you? "No."

Computer workshop schedule.

Nintendo 64 Survival Guide 2, by J. Douglas Arnold.

Printer advice.

Copier advice.

"You got the criminal acts book?"

Internet signups: 45

Friday, October 31, 2003

In the Morning

Macbeth, "the one with the best actors, and the play as well."

Brief HTML design advice. "You mean you can pull in pictures from other places?"

"Who wrote *How to Tie Ties?*"

I'm sure, ma'am, that the books on vitamins will list foods high in vitamin D.

Printer advice, before he tells me he has no money to print.

Printer advice. She was charged for a blank page.

Drowning Ruth, by Christina Schwarz.

Speak, by Laurie Halse Anderson.

Some child abuse statutes, but the customer grows bored and wanders off.

Printer advice.

Printer advice.

I lose a customer over the phone.

Printer advice.

Computer crash.

The Four Agreements, by don Miguel Ruiz.

"I need to know who wrote the classical song 'Bohemian Rhapsody.'"

She wants to download a 49MB device driver onto her floppy.

Copier advice. (The paper comes out here . . . not on the side . . . no, look down, ma'am . . . down . . .)

Nearby Masonic temple

In the Afternoon

Where can he get something laminated?

Newspapers for the last three days.

Go Tell It on the Mountain, by James Baldwin.

Chess books.

Value Line, and how late we're open today.

Can I help you find something? "Health." Can you narrow it down? "Diet." Any type of diet? "Atkins." Perfect.

E.A.R.L., by DMX and Smokey D. Fontaine.; and books by Zane.

Sunday's paper.

Stapler.

Any book by Gabriel García Márquez.

Copier advice.

Holds at the front desk, sir. And don't run. I don't care if you are 72 years old and full of zest.

A child at the new books makes an evil noise.

Copier advice.

Printer advice.

CABCO building codes, which no one around here uses.

"I need information on this person." She points to "Jacobean Age" on her syllabus.

Printer advice.

Printer advice.

Printer advice. He finally triumphs with the color copy option!

Phone number for a local department store.

Caravans, by James Michener.

Holds at the front desk, sir. Yes, sir, that desk there, the one I'm pointing at.

Computer workshop schedule.

I hate last-minute rushes on Fridays.

Chapter 6

Why Are These People in the Library?

"THE LIBRARY: PEOPLE'S UNIVERSITY OR SOCIAL SERVICE CENTER"

From April 1989 to February 1991, I wrote a column titled "Using Technology" for the now defunct *Wilson Library Bulletin.* In the March 1990 issue, I listed six visions of possible library developments in the year 2020. Here is a summary of one of these visions:

> All existing public library buildings have been converted to social service agencies. However, the social service offered is not quite the same as it was in the 1980s. The library social service centers are the places citizens who need to interact in some way with their government can visit and actually receive the needed help or information, cheerfully and without red tape. . . . sleeping centers for the temporarily homeless (a problem still persisting) are located in all department stores (which were also nationalized and replaced by home computer shopping access in 2011). (Anderson, 1990, p. 92)

Given the way that a number of public libraries are now used by the homeless, particularly libraries that have open access to Internet terminals, I am willing to admit that I was wrong about the homeless. Some public libraries with online access and other entertainment media such as plasma screen displays now have become the place

Reference Librarianship: Notes from the Trenches
© 2006 by The Haworth Press, Inc. All rights reserved.
doi:10.1300/5672_06

to spend the day for many homeless individuals. This is confirmed not only by personal observation but also, with a few exceptions, by comments on the subject from librarian subscribers to a public library e-mail list. Other comments indicated that, as tax support for treatment and care facilities dwindled, the public library became a destination of choice for adult groups of mentally challenged individuals as well as people with mental disturbances. All of these situations impose additional stresses in providing traditional library reference service.

Historically, in any depression, when unemployment increases, people have turned to the free public library for information. Also in a historical context, the American public library has been seen as the "People's University." Although we are not facing a depression at this point, one might think that the recent recession would have driven more temporarily unemployed workers to the library. Rather, superficial observations suggest that besides the homeless using public-access terminals, a number of people visit the library not to access traditional information services but rather as a site for free access to e-mail and Web browsing, including pornography. Of course, under the broadest definition, casual Web browsing, as well as specific searches and even e-mail, could be considered as "information-seeking behavior."

One question that may surface among those responsible for library direction is whether the clientele for in-house use is the real target audience for library support. Are the in-house users likely voters in library taxation/bond issues? Exactly who is the target audience for library services beyond the use of the book collection? Except possibly for preschool story hours and students, perhaps many affluent library users now come to libraries just to pick up books they have reserved over the Internet or to find the latest best sellers. If people are not interested in, or do not have the time for, casual in-library browsing for reading needs, then cheap storefront operations to supply reserved books and the latest hot items might make more economic sense than building six-figure downtown library monuments.

When I visit my local library branch, with its room-filled reserve pickup center, often more people are waiting in line to check out books than are sitting around using in-house resources—with the exception of the Internet access terminals. This observation is repeatable at other branches. A bit of statistical computation based on circulation and book stock data from this branch suggests the turnover rate (circulation divided by volumes) is more than twice that of the library system as a whole. The in-house collection, at least from an inspection by an experienced librarian, is not anything remarkable, and the obviously overflowing shelves of books awaiting pickup add some evidence that at least in one major system, one prime attraction and use of local libraries is access to a large system-wide collection rather than individual branch holdings. Could savings be realized by cutting out what is in a sense a middle-person? That is, why not follow the marketing strategy of Amazon.com and ship books directly to the end user?

Obviously, libraries across the country differ in use patterns. For example, some places with substantial genealogical collections will have heavy use of resources, with customers spending the entire day on research. However, if one significant use of a number of libraries is as a homeless or mentally-challenged shelter, is there not a better way to solve these needs than multimillion-dollar new libraries? Or, as one administrator asked, "Have libraries become the asylum?"

The way that public libraries are now used, and the way that they may be used in the next ten to twenty years, would seem to be major factors in the design of new libraries. Is it really good stewardship of tax money to rebuild a library every five to ten years? Unfortunately, as a librarian and interested taxpayer, it is somewhat difficult to see that these future considerations have received much attention in the design of some new libraries.

Beyond library design questions, there is clearly a great need for information services in the social life of the community. Library staff are not trained to provide social services any more than they are trained to provide legal or medical services. The best librarians can do is provide information in each of these areas when needed. They can do more by becoming more active in community outreach. However, if library administrative decisions emphasize circulation above all other library roles (which will require either ever-larger expenditures for self-checkout systems plus perhaps automated materials handling systems or a greater commitment to circulation staff with a concurrent decrease in reference staff) who will have time to provide information services to our multifaceted population? Will the Web—even though a good case could be made that the new People's University is the Web itself—be an adequate substitute for traditional library information services?

📖   📖   📖

A GRUNT'S DIARY: NOVEMBER 2003

Monday, November 03, 2003

In the Afternoon

I butt into Librarian Q's ref interview—a bad habit of mine.

Can I help you? "No."

I am overly nice to an attractive customer.

Printer advice.

Printer advice.

Computer workshop info.

State tax form online link doesn't work, she says. She is wrong.

Suzanne's Diary for Nicholas, by James Patterson.

Oh god, a "Twilight Zone" cell-phone ringer.

Diary of a Groupie, by Omar Tyree.

They'll make change at the front desk, sir.

1999 Ford Expedition repair manual.

Bathroom.

What are our local papers?

In the Evening

Stapler.

Chrysler's business strategies.

Yearbooks.

"Mi Vida Loca," by "El Loco." "It's about gangsters." When I show him the Rodriguez book he rejects it.

Printer advice.

Local black history info.

Citizenship forms.

Dating Games, by R. M. Johnson, *Trouble Man,* by Travis Hunter, and *Diary of a Groupie,* by Omar Tyree.

"Books by Carol Joyce Oates."

Librarian W reports that a customer claims that fairies stole his hat.

Today's paper.

1 John 3:17.

Local driving ordinances.

Lesko books. Happily she wanted it for school money, so I showed her other sources.

Let me show you how to place holds, sir.

A customer left a blue folder here two weeks ago.

Meanwhile, someone forgot their scarf.

Copier advice.

Internet signups: 15

Tuesday, November 11, 2003

In the Afternoon

"Greek mythology. . . . They had people with wings, right?"

Missing wallet.

A lot of city directories.

Missing volumes of *Transmetropolitan.* I'm pissed off about it, too.

How to write short stories.

Tattoo books.

Sorry, sir, no one at the parole office told us anything about a court order to keep your stepson from looking at vodou sites on the Web.

Gossip Girl books, and *The A-List,* by Zoey Dean.

Copier advice.

Coin and paper money collecting.

Sorry, you have to be older than nine to use the computer, little girl.

Missing floppy.

Houseplants.

Copier advice. I hate the new copier.

Alcorn State transcripts.

Government job Web sites.

Microfilm machine advice.

"Jewish cookbooks."

Poetry.

Medical dictionary.

Rubber band, or tape.

Sorry, you have to be more than eleven to use the computers up here, little girl.

Renew your card at the front desk, sir.

Our bi-yearly request for a TTY phone.

Don't run!

"Teen poetry."

The Big Bad Wolf, by James Patterson.

Internet signups: 11

Thursday, November 13, 2003

In the Morning

"Do you speak Spanish?"

Automobile body work.

She can't figure out an online college catalog. . . . Neither can I.

Copier advice.

Driving directions, in great detail.

Librarian Y and I discuss the weather.

Can I help you? "No."

Librarian Y and I discuss digital cameras.

Printer advice.

Printer advice.

Computer crash.

Today's papers.

Computer crash.

Printer advice.

Librarian Y and I discuss Lene Lovich.

"Is Bob there?" Bob?

Today's paper.

The Republic, by Plato.

Computer workshop info.

In the Afternoon

The Lovely Bones, by Alice Sebold.

Local zoning ordinances.

"Medical billing."

Notarization.

Computer crash.

Scram, kid.

It's 3:20, sir.

Of Mice and Men, by John Steinbeck.

"The resolution on my screen just went, like, totally huge."

Love poetry.

Jacobean age.

Pencil and paper, and don't call me buddy.

Skin care and nutrition.

Pimples? Yes, sir. Oh, you said pit bulls. Sorry.

Computer crash.

Computer crash.

Off these machines, kids.

Edgar Allan Poe.

Yearbooks.

Copier advice.

More pit bulls.

Pen.

They'll make change at the front desk, kid.

Copier advice.

Police academies.

We find his missing floppy. "My whole life is on this disk." I suggest he make a backup.

WPs are over there, sir.

That's all the scratch paper we have, kid, and don't run!

Home remodeling.

Home appliance repair.

Wells? You mean the things to draw water out of? Oh, whales. Sorry.

Internet signups: 39

Friday, November 14, 2003

In the Morning

Printer advice.

The AV room is downstairs, ma'am.

1992 Mazda 929 repair manual.

"Has so-and-so signed up for the computer?" Sorry, ma'am, I can't give out that information. "Fuck you." (Click)

We put your notebook in the lost and found, sir.

Why is this man telling me about *The Weakest Link?*

"The history of a jacket."

Harry Potter and the Prisoner of Azkaban, on tape.

Does MapQuest do Mexico?

Printer advice.

Printer advice.

Two notarizations.

I don't think he cares which anti-Bush book he gets, just so he gets one.

ASVAB book.

APA style manual.

In the Afternoon

A lousy, stinking salesman.

There's another copier downstairs, sir.

Newspapers.

WPs are over there, ma'am.

Some *Ultimate X-men* volumes.

WPs are over there, ma'am.

Printer advice.

Sorry, sir, no food in the library.

African Laughter, by Doris Lessing, and *The Lion on the Path,* by Hugh Tracey.

"Is so-and-so there?" Sorry, ma'am, I can't give out that information. "Oh that's okay. Thank you!" (Click)

The Bean Trees, by Barbara Kingsolver.

A Raisin in the Sun, by Lorraine Hansberry.

"I want to know if you got this book." What book? "I just forgot. . . ."

Internet signups: 20

Tuesday, November 18, 2003

In the Morning

Do you have an e-mail account, sir?

Sunday paper.

The copier needs money, ma'am.

Salmonella.

I tell the man three times that we don't have carbon paper. He just stares at me.

Printer advice.

It's hard to explain Internet login procedure when your customer is deaf.

Printer advice.

Printer advice.

Copier advice.

Baby name books.

I can't make the text any bigger, ma'am.

Printer advice.

The Gentrys: Cal, by Linda Conrad.

"My mom wants books by Christina Agathy. She writes books like Sherlock Holmes."

Pen.

Stapler.

Pen.

Newspaper from last week.

City directory.

Another city directory.

Stop calling me "dear."

WPs are over there, ma'am.

That woman is going to bug the man sitting at the machine next to her for advice until he explodes.

A batch of newspapers.

"Self-help books on tape."

Cry No More, by Linda Howard.

Printer advice.

I help a woman over the phone. Meanwhile the line forms. They are all impatient. One is sighing dramatically. One is tapping his fingers on the counter. Another hangs his head. Others exchange meaningful looks concerning the decline of service in modern society. It is the best display of put-uponness that I've seen in some time. I find it so amusing I almost neglect to call Librarian X for backup.

In the Afternoon

Marriage proposals. The customer's sister wants to propose at a dinner in front of both families and wants ideas. A fun reference question!

Pregnancy.

A customer screams and has a fit.

Today's paper.

Pen.

What Librarian Q said on the phone: "Yes, ma'am, we have outlets if you want to plug in your laptop here." What the customer heard: "Yes ma'am, bring in the carcass of your PC here and we'll diagnose your hard-drive problems for you."

Printer advice.

Sorry, you're too young for the Internet, kid.

Ah, the paramedics are here.

Missing floppy.

CEO of Hallmark Cards.

The paramedics wheel out the customer, who is looking much better.

Today's paper.

Printer advice.

What a Wonderful World, by Bob Thiele.

Today's paper.

Today's paper.

Today's paper.

Library Y wonders who is taller: Simon or Garfunkel?

The Adventures of Tom Sawyer, by Mark Twain. "The new version."

Copier advice.

Today's paper.

Stuff by Richard Wilbur, but I suspect the customer is confused.

Batteries, and "lemon power."

Cookbooks. I try to have him narrow it down, I really do!

State tax forms.

Computer virus software.

Printer advice.

1987 Mercury Sable repair manual.

Internet signups: 35

Wednesday, November 19, 2003

In the Afternoon

I do not feel well at all today.

A Feast for Crows, by George R. R. Martin.

Printer advice.

You need a photo ID to use the computers, ma'am.

I give my "How to use the microfilm reader" speech.

Printer advice.

Lost floppy.

Oh, my stomach . . .

Library cards at the front desk, ma'am.

Phone book.

Stapler.

Madame X, the one with Lana Turner.

Push the green button, ma'am.

You spelled "yahoo" wrong, sir.

"I need a historical novel and a book on somebody's life."

Local paper.

Log-in problems.

No, I don't know why that page won't load, ma'am.

Address to the American Cancer Society.

Newspapers for October.

Sorry, I don't know what reference book you were looking at earlier.

Old yearbooks.

Old city directories.

Add about a half-dozen computer crashes to the above. I'm going home to bed.

Internet signups: 43

Friday, November 21, 2003

In the Morning

"Moody's Dividend Manual"

Here's a catalog right here, sir.

Online citizenship exam.

Devil's Canyon, by Ralph Compton.

"Does the *Wall Street Journal* have a business section?"

Congressman's phone number.

Microfilm reader explanation.

Where's the big meeting? In the meeting room.

Today's paper.

Two paper jams.

Copier advice.

How to reply to an e-mail.

Sunday's paper.

Yesterday, both copiers were being repaired. Today, they are both broken.

"English language encyclopedias."

"I'm finished with the paper!" She's taken each section from the pole and mixed the pages up.

1996 Hyundai Excel repair manual.

Night, by Elie Wiesel.

Computer crash.

Washroom?

"Where's the working copy machines?"

Texas Rich, by Fern Michaels.

Internet signups: 26

Monday, November 24, 2003

In the Afternoon

The phone request listed a woman's name, last known address, and Social Security number. I think we're supposed to find her.

"Got anything by William Blake?"

The Da Vinci Code, by Dan Brown.

Screenplay format.

Phone number for the local megacorporation.

Today's paper.

Car price guides.

Indiana Department of Motor Vehicles.

Local naval base.

Flipped, by Wendelin Van Draanen.

Insurance fraud.

In the Evening

His browser won't accept cookies.

Printer advice.

Dylan Thomas.

"Books on diffusion."

Blue screen of death.

Today's paper.

Montezuma.

Crum, by Lee Maynard.

Library cards at the front desk, sir.

Today's paper.

The Raccoon Next Door, by Gary Bogue and Chuck Todd.

Behold a Pale Horse, by William Cooper, and books on Egyptian mythology.

Who keeps taking the "Out of Order" sign off the copier?

Internet signups: 20

Wednesday, November 26, 2003

In the Morning

"Are you open tomorrow?" asks one of our homeless.

Baby name books in Spanish.

Fathers' Rights, by Jeffery M. Leving.

Washroom?

Printer advice.

More printer advice for the same customer.

(Sigh) And still more. I learn that Chuck E. Cheese owes him money.

Printer advice for a different customer.

September newspapers.

English Standard Version Bible.

A listing of people who have just moved here.

"Can I renew a book from another library here?"

He calls asking for a 2002 issue of *Consumer Reports* for the second time.

In the lobby a baby is tortured, possibly in observance of Thanksgiving.

In the Afternoon

I get threatened by three men when I tell them to keep it down. Happy Thanksgiving!

Newspapers from 2001.

Coin collecting.

Try the kids' section.

Printer advice.

Sorry, sir, all the Internet machines are taken. Please stop whining.

Every Second Counts, by Lance Armstrong.

The kid is singing "Twinkle twinkle" loudly and incessantly. The mother is looking for tapes on anger management.

No sleeping in the library, sir.

I have your floppy right here, ma'am.

Kids' section is downstairs, sir.

Internet signups: 47

Saturday, November 29, 2003

In the Morning

Pen.

"Neck anatomy," and books by John McDougall.

Can I help you? "No."

Sorry sir, we don't have an obit index for the 1970s. Oh yes, we do for that year, but we don't have that issue of the paper available.

Microfilm machine lecture and demo.

Today's paper.

Library programs for December and January.

Printer advice.

Notarization.

Copier advice.

Librarian W is on a break but should be back soon, ma'am.

Value Line.

Copier advice.

I lug out a bunch of yearbooks and city directories, knowing in my heart that they will not be the ones the customer needs.

Address, phone for state senators.

Another guy wants state senators.

Donald Goines books.

It sounds like you need a device driver, sir, but I don't know which one your laptop needs.

The catalog is right there, sir.

Today's paper.

Roman cathedrals.

A mysterious form needs to be downloaded.

Of Mice and Men, by John Steinbeck.

Betrothed, by Allesandro Manzoni.

"Did anyone nearby win the lottery on the 26th of this month?"

"I need two books on drugs and violence."

Copier advice.

Today's paper.

Don't run!

In the Afternoon

Printer advice.

Copier advice (It needs money, sir).

Printer advice.

Newspaper.

I draw a blank on three books. But I do find *The Wedding,* by Nicholas Sparks.

Comcast customer service number.

"Do you got a book called *Astrology?*"

Old almanacs? Sorry.

The restroom is over there, sir. He decides to tell me the joke about renting coffee.

Pen.

Newspaper.

We close at five, sir.

Computer workshop info.

Spell books. "You got one to make a person nicer?"

Sorry, ma'am, you can't check out newspapers.

"This place is dank," he says, and exits.

Value Line.

Stapler.

She picks them off a list: "Books on AIDS, alcoholism, and cancer."

1989 Ford Taurus repair manual.

White Christmas, by Jody Rosen.

Internet signups: 31

Chapter 7

Reference Questions

"I NEED HELP!"

"My boyfriend's brother is in jail, and I want to find out why."

"I want some sixth-sense books, and I think it's called metaphysics."

"I'm trying to locate the place where my sister drowned."

"The bank where my account resided in 1977 is no longer there. Where did my money go?"

"I need books on business management and the rules of engagement."

"I'd like some books on the Kama Sutra and also books on starting a home business."

"I need to find a book I read before about enzymes. The cover is green."

"I remember a book called Alternative medicine. *It's thick. Do you have it?"*

"Do you have books to clean up your heart without surgery?"

"My child has something called 'Gerb.' Do you have any books on this?"

"I need the textbook definition of 'decision making.' "

Reference Librarianship: Notes from the Trenches
© 2006 by The Haworth Press, Inc. All rights reserved.
doi:10.1300/5672_07

"Reference anxiety," although not recognized in the *Diagnostic and Statistical Manual of Mental Disorders,* is nevertheless a real factor in serving on a public library reference desk (Anderson, 2003). These examples of real questions are the kinds of things that reference librarians are confronted with on a daily basis. Granted, not every question at an information desk may present with the sense of immediacy or tragedy that these particular questions exemplify.

However, for every person who needs a consumer report for washers, dryers, cameras, hot water heaters, camcorders, and so on, or asks where are the mysteries, Bruce Lee books, parenting books, business career books, books on J-Lo, books like Laura Ingalls Wilder, and so on, you never know when the next questioner will want to know how to cope with nightmares.

Professionals in the health care fields soon learn to objectify their clients. Doctors, nurses, psychologists, and others who work daily with people having real or imagined but important ailments, have to disassociate themselves from any real bonding with their patients or risk constant psychic assaults. This does not mean that persons in these fields cannot feel sympathy, but entering into any kind of empathetic connection can be dangerous for the caregiver's mental health.

Can or should reference librarians practice the same objectivity? Will it help librarians provide better service if there is an element of empathy involved in each reference contact—at least those that go beyond the simple questions?

Several significant differences exist between the health care field and reference librarians. For one thing, unlike the health care field, encounters in the library with reference librarians almost certainly are never a life-or-death situation. Nor do reference librarians have a monetary stake in the outcome of any reference transaction. Granted, any reference librarian who fails to answer questions on a regular basis probably risks a monetary loss in salary for not doing his or her job. However, whether or not each individual library user goes away with a good answer, a poor answer, or no answer at all does not affect the daily income of the reference librarian. A health care professional who renders poor, erroneous, or no service at all risks considerable monetary problems and possible malpractice suits.

A third difference is that, of the hundreds or more people who approach a specific reference desk every day, probably only a very few will be repeat customers—at least on more than a weekly or, more likely, monthly basis. This infrequent pattern of contact lessens the personal impact of seeing someone who desperately needs sources of financial aid or help with child sexual abuse problems.

These typical limitations on exposure of reference librarians to in-depth psychic contact with customers are inherent in the existential nature of reference transactions. Furthermore, the largely unrecognized philosophical orientation of both customers and librarians plays an important role in these interactions.

Americans have been characterized as being all nominalists by birth. However, neo-Platonism, which some characterize as the "perennial philosophy," continues to create tensions in our society, as witness recurrent appeals to abstract or transcendent realities such as "patriotism," "duty," or "honor" (Anderson, 1996).

Since reference librarians are a part of our society, these tensions must be endemic in our professional life. The article just referenced attempted to provide a methodology to analyze the existential interactions between customer and librarian using the Kierkegaardian aesthetic, ethical, and religious modalities. The presumption made in that article was that most customers who ask simple, non-basic-life-impacting questions are acting in an aesthetic modality (easier visualized as "spur-of-the-moment"), while customers approaching the reference desk with the type of questions that opened this section tend to be acting in an ethical or religious modality. A simpler way to view these latter modalities and their impact on the reference transaction is to assume that the customer's real personality is, at least at the moment of truth, vitally concerned in the outcome of the conversation, either because their question is of paramount health or quality-of-life importance or it involves deeply-held ethical or religious beliefs.

Although this section is not the place to delve further into these fundamental philosophical questions, the point is that to excel at reference desk work it is sometimes necessary for the librarian to enter more deeply than a superficial level into the customer's world. In other words, to better understand the customer's needs and have a better chance of meeting those needs, more is required than the simple skills promoted by such techniques as the "Four Elements of Reference Transaction Success," that is, "Welcoming, Paraphrasing, Negotiation, Follow-up." Reference librarians need some degree of empathetic transfer to establish effective two-way communication with the customer.

Even with the best intentions in the world and empathetic understanding of customers, the larger question of the future of reference remains. The words "reference work" first appeared in *Library Journal* in 1891. By 1904 Mary Aileen Ahearn, a well-known librarian of the day, said, "the reference work of the library gives the institution its greatest value and may be called the heart of the work. The very best talent obtainable should be placed in the reference room. . . . Here is where the real educative work is done" (Ahern, 1904, p. 55). As noted in other essays in this book and in the literature, reference work is changing in many libraries. By multiple accounts, reference questions are decreasing while circulation is rising. The Internet as yet does not seem to be an adequate substitute for experienced reference librarians, even though it appears that significant numbers of the public may think it is.

Doing a Google search on a term and looking at the first ten hits may at times seem to answer the customer's question, but there is no guarantee that the answer will be as authoritative as that furnished by a professional trained to evaluate sources and retrieve information. Perhaps, as Web search software improves, this may change, but for the foreseeable future, I believe we still will need reference librarians. The big question is whether library administrators who are seeking the most obvious statistical proof of the library's worth—circulation—will continue to believe this.

📖 📖 📖

A GRUNT'S DIARY: DECEMBER 2003

Monday, December 1, 2003

In the Afternoon

Value Line.

Divorce records in Ohio.

Catholic directory.

Yes, ma'am, we have outlets for laptops.

Value Line. Not that one, the other one.

Three notarizations.

Copier advice.

"How are you today?" Then she pauses and actually expects you to answer.

Sanctuary, by Faye Kellerman.

Who's Looking Out for You, by Bill O'Reilly.

Old newspapers.

"This is So-And-So. How are you?" and another pause. People sure care about my health today. Maybe it's the holiday season.

Dictionary of Occupational Titles.

Sorry, ma'am, you can't check out newspapers.

More old newspapers.

Copier advice.

2002 1040.

In the Evening

Stapler.

Copier advice.

Library cards at the front desk, ma'am.

Pencil.

A man makes some copies and sighs to himself, "Not nice."

Wisconsin phone books. . . . Actually he just needed the address of one lodge.

"Divorce books with forms?"

"What's going on in the meeting room?"

The receptionist transfers a hard question to us: "What time you close today?"

Notarization.

Today's paper.

"The middle colonies."

Henry Ford.

You're too young to use the computers up here, kid.

"The history of World War II . . . and books on building a house . . . and Spanish-English dictionaries."

Copier advice.

Paperback fiction is over here, sir.

A microfilm reader goes kerflooey. There's film all over the carpet.

The Reverse of the Medal, and *The Far Side of the World,* by Patrick O'Brian.

Microfilm printer jam.

Address for two radio stations.

Washroom.

Lowriders.

Hairstyling books.

AV room is downstairs, sir.

"How much is 50 ounce of fine silver nowadays?

Internet signups: 14

Thursday, December 4, 2003

In the Afternoon

Butter.

I am told that I am not scheduled on desk.

In the Evening

Pen.

How much snow we're going to get.

"The printer is copying out sideways."

Immigration law.

Marijuana books.

I don't think the study room will fit all eight of you.

The customer is disappointed because the newspaper article about his arrest doesn't have his picture.

"A dictionary of old English words." Actually they just need help with a Tennyson poem.

Large print Bible.

AV calls. A woman needs music she could "act out," or just listen to. I'm not sure what she wants, and I hope she doesn't come to this desk (She doesn't).

I like a slow shift.

Thursday, December 11, 2003

In the Morning

He shoves a book in my hands. "This is yours."

Currency trading, and he won't shut up.

Don't run (3 times)!

She left a document in the copier last night. . . .

He's surprised I can't appraise a book for him.

1991 Toyota Camry repair manual.

Italian-English dictionaries.

In the Afternoon

Gwendolyn Brooks.

"*Carnival of Dreams,*" but whether a book, CD, what, he doesn't know.

They jump up and down. "We want devil books!" "Yeah! devil books!"

Local phone book.

"Excuse me sir. I am told by the gentleman over there that you are the gods and gurus of information on my particular . . ." Will you ask the damn question already?

You can plug in a laptop over there, ma'am.

Sorry sir, I haven't seen your bag of medication.

Dave Pelzer books in Spanish.

Throwing Christmas parties.

How to recharge a debit card.

A customer thanks me. I forget what I did for her.

Today's paper.

Lit crit for "We Wear the Mask," by Paul Laurence Dunbar.

Storm Warriors, by Elisa Carbone.

"Books on Excel, Access, Lotus, you know . . ."

"Short Order Cook," by Jim Daniels.

Don't run!

He actually wants an AOL start-up disk.

Local directions.

Internet signups: 31

Friday, December 12, 2003

In the Morning

Librarian Y warns me about a woman at the copier.

A swarm of new customers from the Philippines.

Christmas cookies.

A swarm of old customers gets impatient while I help the new customers. The three computer crashes didn't help.

In Hotmail, "Compose" now reads "New Message," confusing one customer.

1991 Honda Accord repair manual.

Ours is the "most complete library" he's ever been in.

Copier advice.

A brusque, twelve-foot-tall man orders me to find him law books, but at least he doesn't threaten me.

I hear an Internet customer say "Argh." I save the day.

Debit card machine is over there, sir.

1993 Chevrolet van repair manual.

Printer advice.

The woman at the copier, who has ignored all my advice and squandered over a dollar, wants her money back.

Screwy display settings.

Piano keyboard technique.

Old Mac books.

Ford engine overhaul.

Sorry, sir, no typewriter.

That woman is still on the copier. I warn Librarian X.

In the Afternoon

MacWrite Pro books.

Notary forms.

Local charity phone.

1992 Chevy Cavalier repair manual, especially the cooling system.

"Monster books?"

I sneak away to rent DVDs for the weekend.

"Robot books?"

Today's paper.

Today's paper.

Sorry ma'am, we can't reserve study rooms in advance. Sure, I'll let you speak to the department head. . . .

Christmas in Belize.

There must be a Chicken Soup book for Christmas. . . .

A request for a Social Security form interrupts my discussion with Techie X about Sarah Michelle Gellar and Scooby Doo.

I Make My Own Rules, by LL Cool J.

Today's paper.

Simpsons books.

Looking for her daughter . . .

Internet signups: 47

Monday, December 15, 2003

In the Afternoon

Australopithecus boisei.

Sunday's paper.

WPs are over there, sir.

They try to kill a porn site and two more take its place.

Try switching machines, ma'am.

I debug a password problem.

Alone on the desk, and the customer has never used a mouse before and wants info on trucks, "what you can do with them."

Pencil.

We no longer carry that database, sir.

What's that default screen doing there?

"What aisle's the poems?"

Pencil.

Hemingway books.

She insists it's the "Small Business Association," and wanders off empty handed.

Printer advice.

Printer advice.

Copier not working . . . whoops, yes it is.

Criss-Cross.

Printer advice.

Leyes Eternas, by Carlos Cuauhtemoc Sanchez.

"My computer froze."

Swamp Thing on DVD.

Computer crash or three.

Meanwhile that child just keeps hacking up phlegm.

In the Evening

Eddings and Poe.

Periodic table.

Stairs are over there, sir.

Arrogance, by Bernard Goldberg, and *Journalistic Fraud,* by Bob Kohn.

The Color of Water, by James McBride.

Donald Goines books.

Copier advice.

Printer advice.

Out of the stacks, kids.

1978-1979 yearbook.

Sue Johanson.

1977-1978 yearbook.

"A Whole New World," on CD, but they must have an instrumental version.

Paper jam.

Sorry sir, I can't extend a loan on an ILL.

Don't run!

Postage meter?

Today's paper.

Books on The Flash. He settles for JLA books.

Marathon running.

Horse books in Spanish.

Pro wrestling books.

"What time do you close?" Right now.

Internet signups: 62

Tuesday, December 16, 2003

In the Morning

Stapler.

WPs are over there, ma'am.

Pencil.

Microfilm reader advice (turn that knob the other way, sir).

Printer advice.

WPs are over there, sir.

Phone book.

Beauty salon phone.

Reboot.

Vehicle emissions testing station phone.

Eric Jerome Dickey books, and *Kiss the Girls,* by James Patterson.

Audiobook policy question.

In the Afternoon

Whole bunch of articles to ILL. She's coughing all over the forms.

Local power company phone.

Techie Y, a computer genius, stops by to pick up an "Out of Order" sign. That can't be good.

Password problem.

A speech delivered "after they bombed the tiny town of London for sixty straight days." He then tells Librarian Q she looks like Winston Churchill.

Science of whirlpools.

"A book by Masquesz. I think that's how it's spelled."

"Werewolves, the psychological aspect."

WPs are over there, ma'am.

"Let me go!" shouts the child.

She forgot to write down the book's bib info while she was here.

There are kids stuck in the elevator.

Internet signups: 36

Thursday, December 18, 2003

In the Morning

Librarian Y gives me copier advice.

Stapler.

Old newspapers to give away?

Local map.

Today's paper.

Our pencil sharpener is busted.

Printer advice.

Another customer gives me sad doe eyes when I won't help her format her document.

Father holds baby. Baby smiles. Mother holds baby. Baby screams.

Today's paper.

Local history books.

In the Afternoon

Bureau of Indian Affairs number. "Oh, never mind, I found it."

ILL loan extension.

Criss-Cross.

Someone's stuck in the elevator, just ringing that bell. . . .

My computer crashes.

Why Do Clocks Run Clockwise? by David Feldman.

The Glass Menagerie, by Tennessee Williams.

They're kids' books, so I can get rid of the caller by transferring her.

Librarian Y and I team up and answer a question with great efficiency because the customer is loud and annoying.

Property tax posting.

"I'm looking for information on my ancestors, aunts, great aunts, and everything, and how they fit together, and I don't know anything about using a computer. No, I'm not from this town."

WPs are over there, ma'am.

Internet signups: 30

Friday, December 19, 2003

In the Morning

Copier advice.

Poetry books.

Blow Fly, by Patricia Cornwell.

Put away your stupid cell phone.

Tip for library students: When a customer asks for a particular yearbook, also bring them the years before and after. Trust me.

You can buy a floppy at the front desk, sir.

Stapler.

"Is Techie Y there?"

Today's paper.

Bird guides.

The Big Bad Wolf, by James Patterson.

State employment office.

Article in an old newspaper, maybe on a Monday . . .

Printer advice.

In the Afternoon

Printer advice

Immigration forms.

"Oh, just got out of jail. Everything good with you?"

We'll reshelve that for you, ma'am.

Today's paper.

"Is Librarian Q there?"

County courthouse phone.

Exercise, "especially the belly."

Sorry ma'am, I can't tell you who's on the Internet.

Car repair.

The man is fascinated by his problems with the copier and tells everyone at length.

Southwestern design.

Today's paper.

Today's paper.

"Merry Christmas." Sure, why the hell not?

Yes, you can use a computer, but we're about to close.

Printer advice.

Internet signups: 21

Monday, December 22, 2003

In the Afternoon

Fiction?

Any working copiers?

Pictures of penguins.

Where are the YA books?

The spelling of Buddha.

Any working copiers?

"Everybody's so busy reading . . ."

"Do you offer any classes besides computers?"

Today's paper.

In the Evening

Working copier?

The argument over a damaged book has gone on for over twenty minutes.

Resume books.

Criss-Cross.

A man sneakily looks at porn on the Internet.

A woman gets too wacky with the "Undo" function. I manage to fix it.

Map of Nevada.

Fan information for The Box Tops.

His ILL hasn't arrived yet.

It's past closing. A woman on a WP is shouting at the poor Internet girl because she won't help edit her document.

Internet signups: 11

Tuesday, December 23, 2003

In the Morning

What's at that address?

Map reading.

Can I help you? "No."

Techie X says a man is doing something sneaky on one Internet terminal, but we can't figure out what.

"Tax forms out yet?"

A man wants to catch up with the Wheel of Time series.

They accidentally bring up a porn Web page. They think it's so funny they show it to everyone.

A law office has moved.

How to get to Yahoo! when there's a pdf file on the screen.

"I'm an idiot when it comes to computers."

In the Afternoon

Today's paper.

Any book by Zane.

Horse racing.

The Tao of Pooh, by Benjamin Hoff.

Floppies at the front desk, sir.

Alice Walker.

"Can I do public service there?"

A video from India I can't locate.

Dictionary. When I use "sir" I at least try to make it sound respectful. . . .

Yellow pages.

Coin books.

That's okay, sir. I'll shelve them for you. You're obviously deranged or on drugs (I didn't really say that).

Today's paper.

Bridget Jones's Diary, by Helen Fielding.

Happy holidays. See you (argh) Saturday.

Internet signups: 18

Monday, December 29, 2003

In the Afternoon

City directories going back to the 1930s, in 5-year intervals.

Computer workshop schedule.

Pen. We're out.

Tax forms.

Sunday paper.

Don't run!

Bible.

Illustrations of camels. "I want to get a head start on next year. I nearly got the manger laid out. We gotta get back to the true meaning of Christmas."

More city directories.

"I know three girls there are on your computers looking at *Playboy,* and it's disgusting. I'm coming in to take care of business."

The time.

Still more city directories, and a topographical map. If the customer wasn't so cute I'd be annoyed.

Grizzly, starring Christopher George.

Career tests.

WPs? Over there.

Books by the Pope.

Yellow pages.

"Is (a customer) there?"

Local shelter. A second homeless guy helps us find it.

Miniature houses.

How to make pottery.

"Any chance you getting the paper card catalogs back anytime soon?"

Audrey Hepburn.

The Da Vinci Code, by Dan Brown, *The Big Bad Wolf,* by James Patterson, and *Is Paris Burning?* by Larry Collins.

More city directories, for a different customer.

Microfilm.

Pencils.

How to turn on the microfilm reader.

Missing floppy.

CLEP exams for microeconomics.

Spanish instruction CDs.

Tax forms.

Stapler.

How to reset the microfilm reader.

In the Evening

You're too young to use the Internet up here, kid.

Catalog reboot.

Vikki Vanishes, by Peni R. Griffin.

The Oakland Athletics team roster.

Coming of Age in Mississippi, by Anne Moody, and *Go Tell It on the Mountain,* by James Baldwin.

Two giggling teen girls want "physical education" (i.e., sex) books.

A calm teen girl wants witchcraft books, including *Wicca Covens,* by Judy Harrow.

Conde Nast Traveller magazine.

Don't run!

And shut up!

River God, by Wilbur Smith.

E-mail addresses for Herbie Hancock, Bill Cosby, Richard Pryor, Sam Kinnison, and Men at Work.

Pencil.

The microfilm machine ate five dimes.

Soulmates Dissipate, by Mary B. Morrison.

Catapults and siege warfare.

He needs more Anne McCaffrey.

Internet signups: 18

Chapter 8

Policy Questions

"WHY DOES (DOESN'T) THE LIBRARY . . ."

As an entertainment medium, library board meetings can range from high drama to low comedy to stultifying boredom. At their worst, one could apply Dorothy Parker's comment on Katherine Hepburn's performance in *The Lake:* "She ran the gamut of emotions from A to B." At their most electrifying, library staff can sit frozen to chairs as they listen to a group of laypersons, often political appointees, who may range from good-hearted souls to personal-ego-development specialists, decide the future direction of multimillion dollar library operations.

In general, when customers ask the question in the title of this section, the real answer is traceable back to the library board, which normally sets policy for library operations. This can be a good thing, or it can be a bad thing. In reading the rest of this section, please keep in mind that sometimes it is necessary to paint in broad strokes—to look at some worst possible scenarios that may illustrate what can go wrong in public library governance. The examples that follow are not completely fictional; instead, they are an amalgam of real or rumored events. As the movies say, any resemblance to real people is coincidental!

For one example, take a hypothetical case in which a library is thinking about the possibility of erecting a massive downtown library (this is a somewhat common event). Simple human nature suggests that civic pride and the realization that this will be a monument not only for the citizens but also for all connected with the project, especially the board, may become part of the deliberations and planning. Perhaps the new library will replace a decaying central library, largely

Reference Librarianship: Notes from the Trenches
© 2006 by The Haworth Press, Inc. All rights reserved.
doi:10.1300/5672_08

populated by the homeless using public access to the Internet, with no parking except expensive commercial spaces and limited public transportation access. There may be a branch system, heavily used by nearby residents, but in trouble with inadequate book budgets. If the library offers the public the chance of a massive bond election to build just a six-figure downtown library in today's economy, the idea may be rejected. If it is, sometimes a dynamic library director can resurrect the project with a second bond election and promises to rescue the branch situation.

As an aside, when I was in library school, one professor solemnly informed us that each librarian would build one library in his or her career. Actually, I participated in the planning for four, so that shows how much that professor knew about the subject. However, I do suspect many library directors harbor the secret fantasy of building a big city, six-figure library as their own monument. Fortunately for the public's tax dollars, few actually get this chance.

Getting back to my hypothetical exposition, what may happen is that this library board and director will develop a plan that will not only get them their monument but also rebuild a number of branches. If you add these promises to the proposal, then the project probably has a better chance of coming to fruition. It has an even better chance if you can run an international competition to find an architect who can present the most unlikely design that is guaranteed to win the plaudits of architectural critics. If all this can be sold to the public, which generally thinks that libraries are a Good Thing, then construction can begin.

For another hypothetical example, imagine a library board that approves the sale of a significant piece of downtown real estate that is currently operating as a centralized library distribution center and headquarters in order to build a new headquarters along one of the most heavily traveled traffic corridors in the area. This new center will cost, with debt-reduction payments and interest included, more than four times the amount realized from the sale. Furthermore, because voter approval of such a project may seem unlikely, if the board is smart it will finance the new building without public approval through a little-known law for issuing bonds. To complete this fictional horror story, which of course could never happen in real life, imagine that it is known the downtown city block sold was within a development area intended to become one of the largest coordinated billion-dollar development areas in the city.

After the reader stops shuddering at these imaginary nightmare scenarios, he or she might wonder whether they actually could happen, or whether less dramatic but consequential mistakes could take place in library decisions. Could major problems with long-term consequences really exist, beyond the myriad stories of board micromanagement, such as going through library staff desks at night or insisting that the library director act as an unpaid chauffeur for the board president (this actually happened to my own knowledge)? The answer is, of course, "It depends."

It depends on the answer to the important question of "Who does an appointed library board represent?" Is it the public? Is it the library staff? Is it the library director? If the previously described situations actually existed, it would be difficult to answer "the public." Fortunately, in many cases, board decisions are made with the best interests of the public in mind. To avoid such potential excesses, it is extremely important that any lay board be very well versed in good library operating principles. If not, the board may become little more than a rubber-stamp committee for the library director. I am not even sure that elected library boards are more answerable to their public. A board member elected for a long term, say six years, may be a bit removed from accountability. In either case, though, the damage that can be done for years in the future by ill-considered actions does exist, even with the best of intentions.

The intentions, whether good or misguided, of library boards, as noted previously, connect directly with the question asked at the beginning of this section, that is, the types of questions that frequently are asked, not of the governing body of a library, but of the frontline staff. "Why does the library allow only fifteen reserves per person?" "Why does the library not subscribe to . . . ?" "Why do I have to turn off my firewall to access one of the library databases?" "Why doesn't the library stay open after nine p.m.?"

These kinds of questions and many more may have answers, but the frontline reference staff probably had no input into the decision-making process that led to the answers. In this, library workers are no different than any other frontline personnel in business operations. Management decides, staff carry out the decisions. Problems arise when library management is able to put into effect policies without the informed discussion that lay board members as well as working staff should bring to the table. A significant responsibility of library management is to educate a library board about the realities of library service.

However, the danger of an educated board is that library administrators may feel their control is weakened. Therefore, depending on where a library administrator falls along the management line of participative to autocratic, the needed board education may not always happen. The absence of a formal process to educate library board members in library philosophy and services is so vital that ignoring this responsibility can cause serious problems.

These problems can include failed projects (and wasted money) that any staff member could have seen were unworkable in the beginning. The kinds of problems that arise from rubber-stamp library boards may even be one cause of successful unionization drives, which may create a whole new set of problems.

This whole situation, of decision making divorced from the realities of library service, probably is the reason that the answer to the "why doesn't the library . . ." question may be simply, "That's the rule," surely one of the most frustrating customer-service responses that exist. However, it is a response that can be found by calling just about any company's customer-service department; therefore, perhaps it is just an ingrained element of "doing business."

Surely, in the business of meeting the public's need for information, there ought to be a better way. . . .

📖   📖   📖

A GRUNT'S DIARY: JANUARY 2004

On January 2 the library adopted a new policy. Customers no longer had to sign up for the Internet and they could stay on as long as they wanted. However, it took awhile for people to figure this out.

Wednesday, January 7, 2004

In the Morning

Bathroom?

The copier can do two sided!

Automatic transmission books in Spanish.

"Gothic poetry," other words he used include "satanic" and "depressing."

Don't run!

She walks by with cell phone in hand: "Hello? . . . Hello? . . . Hello?"

MapQuest can't find her city because it doesn't exist.

Copier advice.

The job Web site comes up for me but not for the customer.

Shut up, kids.

Papers from last week, and a pencil.

Anything new from Sister Souljah since *The Coldest Winter Ever?*

"Excuse me, did you know the mouse is broke?"

Copier advice.

Copier advice (same guy).

Tina Modotti.

In the Afternoon

Copier advice from Techie X.

"Madhouse, madhouse," mutters Librarian Y.

Copier advice (Don't use that machine, sir).

Don't run!

Sorry, ma'am, no fax.

1988 Lincoln repair manual.

Printer advice.

More printer advice.

He wants the creators and storyline for *Annie.*

Pencil.

They want the state as well as the zip code, sir.

No sign-up needed for the Internet: 17

Friday, January 9, 2004

In the Morning

Does it count if someone asks for directions on your way to work?

Internet policy over the phone.

Press enter, sir.

"Ain't you got nothin' with NotePad or WordPad?"

Financial aid books.

Upholstery books.

Pen and paper.

"Has this book reached the library yet, or do I gotta go to a bookstore?" *(The Da Vinci Code)*.

Cayman Islands.

Floor plans.

Today's paper.

Daddy Cool, by Donald Goines.

Printer advice.

Printer advice.

The server forgets about a 23-page document.

Consumer info on gas ranges and refrigerators.

Printer advice.

I play tech support for CompuServe, Windows, and whoever built the customer's CD/RW drive.

How to create an e-mail account.

"That man's been on his cell phone for thirty minutes."

Bel Canto, by Anna Patchett, and *Absolute Friends,* by John Le Carre.

In the Afternoon

Reboot.

"The lady said we could play music in here."

One Thousand White Women, by Jim Fergus.

Notarization.

FAFSA on the Web.

Value Line.

We close at six, sir, and don't sneak up on me like that.

"You can print 1040s off the Web site?" Why are they so amazed?

Restroom. I told you not to sneak up on me.

Sorry, for the last time we're out of Lesko books.

Shut up!

World War II maps.

Last Sunday's paper.

Hinduism.

There's another copier downstairs, sir.

The combination of customer ignorance of computers and their desperate, clinging needs is driving me. . . . Sorry, I'm better now.

Bathroom.

Biopsies.

Blue screen of death.

Click there to place a hold, sir.

Can I help you? (click)

It's getting so I want to strangle even our most sane and reasonable customers. . . .

(Sigh) No, sir, press that button there.

"[giggle] I forgot how to print."

Can you narrow it down at all? We have a lot of "poetry."

"Can I download and print an Adobe pdf document?" Later I have to tell him to click "print."

Dogs, the Ultimate Dictionary of Over 1,000 Dog Breeds, by Desmond Morris.

"Is there a *Kelley's* for firearms?" I'll tell you, sir, if you shut that kid up (I didn't really say that).

Selena.

Auto body parts.

No sign-up needed for the Internet: 15

Tuesday, January 13, 2004

In the Afternoon

How to be a landlord.

I give my microfilm-loading lecture.

I don't know if it was Brian Keith or Brian Dennehy in that movie, sir, if you can't remember the name of the movie.

Knitting books.

Librarian Y and I discuss Atkins.

Every song by Aretha Franklin.

Lodgings near Walt Disney World.

Another microfilm lecture.

Today's paper.

I leave early to teach a class.

Later in the Afternoon

Clown fish.

Books by Thomas Perry.

"It took my dime!" No it didn't, ma'am. Here's your copy right here.

Today's paper.

Military PTSD manual.

A paper we no longer carry.

Librarian M is very nice, but she's very new and needs a lot of help.

Aerial photos of the town.

"The keyboard won't work."

Printer advice.

Sorry ma'am, no zip drives here.

Tax workshop info.

Today's paper.

Printer advice.

A complaint about our Internet policy (at the moment we have none).

"Books on the syllablication and decoding of words. 'Decoding' is breaking a word into syllables."

The bird that, when hatched, pushes all the other eggs out of the nest.

State tax form.

The Holy Greyhound, by Jean-Claude Schmidt, and *Nero,* by Edward Champlin.

Decks and drywall.

Today's paper.

Macroeconomics and a Windows tech support question.

Sunday's paper.

Blue hermit crabs.

I don't know what this lady wants. And the Web site she wants me to try keeps crashing my browser.

Tax forms.

Ionic compounds, or something like that.

2002 yearbooks.

Lawn mower blenny.

Can I help you? "No."

Don't run!

Dream interpretation.

"The local code of ordinances; who wrote it?"

"Where are the poem books?" Also ASVAB guides.

Tax forms are over there, ma'am.

Printer advice.

No signup needed for the Internet: 15

Friday, January 16, 2004

In the Morning

"Good morning." Urgh.

Monet's first name.

"Your network won't let me bid on eBay?" Turn the number lock on, sir.

Printer advice.

Printer advice.

Sometimes you can never figure out what the customer wants, but he's still smiling and nodding at you.

Dinosaurs.

"I want to print this part of the Web page, but not this part."

State tax forms?

Printer advice.

Today's paper.

Books on writing poetry.

Love poetry (different customer).

In the Afternoon

He hates the microfilm reader and tells me all about it.

Study room.

Child torture in the lobby.

Correction fluid, which I run and get from my office because the customer is cute.

That one-year-old can't actually be screaming "No way! Fuck you!" could he?

Writer's Market.

Overheard: "Why do you rap?" "Oh man, I need a job."

It's so quiet I overexplain the online catalog to kill time.

I make the Word format toolbar magically appear. The customer is happy.

He narrows the subject down to water pollution.

Printer advice.

Our security gal is happiest when she gets to ban a customer.

The printer starts to behave when I show up.

I think someone's being sick over there.

I reset the printer again . . .

Tax forms?

The kid shows me the call number "B PEL" and I instantly know what he wants. "How'd you know?"

No sign-up needed for the Internet: 11

Tuesday, January 20, 2004

In the Morning

Sir, if that's a free credit report, why are they asking for a credit card number?

"I need to talk with her. She's in the Internet area, and it's an emergency!"

Copier advice.

Sorry, no fax.

Copier advice.

Printer advice.

Love in the Time of Cholera, by Gabriel García Márquez.

Change is at the front desk, sir.

Local map.

Copier advice.

"What's the Web site for jobs?"

"Which one of these forms is for the state?" Neither, ma'am.

Another state form request.

One Hundred Years of Solitude, by Gabriel García Márquez.

Computer workshop schedule.

You want more copies of the form? There's the copier. Don't get upset with me.

For the third time, sir, press that button there.

Addicted, by Zane.

All about our book discussion groups.

Computer workshop info.

Where to send her election judge stuff.

Phone for a local college.

Nutrition and Physical Degeneration, by Weston A. Price.

Copier advice.

Feng shui videos.

No sign-up needed for the Internet: 5

Wednesday, January 21, 2004

In the Afternoon

Bank statements on the Internet?

Printer advice.

Today's paper.

Two microfilm reader lectures.

Disabled customers and unintuitive online forms do not mix.

Copier advice.

The WPs are over there.

Zoning ordinances.

The final step in filling out the ILL forms, sir, is writing your name.

Science fiction is over there . . . and there.

Charles Dickens.

The spelling of "Burroughs," more than once.

Bipolar disorder. Later, Social Security Insurance books. Then she went back to bipolar.

G. Gordon Liddy.

Songs of the Gorilla Nation, by Dawn Prince-Hughes.

If you want to save that image you'll need a floppy.

"Books on the constitution." Can you narrow it down? "You know, books on it."

"I'm writing a paper about an author: Laura . . . I can't remember."

"No sign-up anymore? Why is that?"

He wants one of our business cards.

"Martial arts books?" he asks with slurring voice.

"Where are the LL's?" asks the child. LL's? "Never mind."

Today's paper.

BlackPlanet.com has one of the most confusing interfaces around.

Math books.

A friendly chat with the director.

Martin Luther King.

Debit card advice.

Isabel Allende.

Colts? The animal? Indianapolis? Baltimore? Oh, Quotes! My bad.

Another customer complains about our Internet policy, or lack of one.

Sorry ma'am, but I can't run down the names and address of all the members of the House of Representatives over the phone.

Two reboots.

Just a guy doing his kid's homework.

A book by Jessica Simpson.

No sign-up needed for the Internet: 11

Thursday, January 22, 2004

In the Morning

Three men stare at the copier.

Washroom?

Visions Across the Americas, by J. Sterling Warner and Judith Hilliard.

The Quarterback, by Terry Shea.

The Lord of the Rings in graphic novel format?

Videos are downstairs, sir.

Three computer workshop schedules.

Scratch paper.

Driver's ed book.

Copier advice.

Here in America's Test Kitchen.

Today's paper.

Men Cry in the Dark, by Michael Baisden, and *Addicted,* by Zane.

Robert's Rules of Order.

Today's paper.

Phone number for someone in Rochester, NY.

No ma'am, I don't know which genealogical Web site would be best for you.

"They said come to the library and go to the jobs Web site."

The new copier is so confusing customers can't even figure out where the copy comes out.

One Hundred Years of Solitude, by Gabriel García Márquez.

The spelling of "Nikki Giovanni" and "Emily Dickinson."

In the Afternoon

Printer advice.

I think he just moved to town and wants all the information there is.

Nicholas Sparks books.

Printer advice and how to cut and paste, more than once. . . .

A customer who's so damn nice you want to throttle her, or at least find her book quickly so she'll go smile at someone else.

Books on alcoholism in Spanish.

I'm getting a sore throat. Is it "a cold is coming" sore throat, or just a sore throat?

The life of Roald Dahl.

The printer is working fine, sir. Here's your copy down here.

Today's paper.

Not completely the same, ma'am. One's a second edition.

Books on Microsoft Word and basic typing.

Dancing Naked, by Shelley Hrdlitschka. Lord, what a name. How do you pronounce that?

A cell phone is missing. I am partly sympathetic, partly relieved.

William Shakespeare.

Photosynthesis.

Stapler.

The Photograph, by Virginia Ellis.

Ma'am, I can't do anything about your fines. You're talking to the wrong department.

Try backspace and not delete, ma'am.

Tax forms.

We close at nine.

Phone book.

The call number is B LLC? Are you sure?

Tax forms.

Stuff about Brianda Domecq, which takes forever.

"Any workshops tonight?"

No sign-up needed for the Internet: 14

Monday, January 26, 2004

In the Evening

Our terminals are packed. There's people waiting, and the whining gets louder every day.

1992 Volvo price.

"You should have a way to get them off the computer so we can get on." He does not define "they" and "we."

Anna Sewell.

Beverly Cleary.

Printer advice.

Three pencils.

Computer workshop info in Spanish.

Stapler.

"Do you have any books with stories about fornication?"

Another Internet policy complaint.

They'll sell you a floppy at the front desk, sir.

She just moved to town and lives in a group home. May she have a library card?

A man stands in front of Librarian W and talks about the Internet for ten minutes, tossing out lines like: "Where's the concept of satisfaction?"

Algebra books.

Mathematics for the Trades, by Robert A. Carman and Hal M. Saunders.

The definition of "thesis."

WPs are over there, sir, well, there are some over there, too.

Meeting room question.

I've never done electronic filing, so I can't tell you, sir.

Criss-Cross.

"Are the computers always this busy?"

Tax forms are over there, sir.

You can buy a debit card over there, ma'am.

Printer advice. The kids are dubious.

Last-minute printer advice.

No sign-up needed for the Internet: 7

Tuesday, January 27, 2004

In the Afternoon

Divorce law.

Five ILL forms.

Online person search.

Copier advice.

Addicted, by Zane, and *Men Cry in the Dark,* by Michael Baisden.

I don't know what immigration form you want, sir.

"I need help with my e-mail."

Librarian X can't come in, so I'm working this evening!

Donald Goines books.

I leave early to teach a workshop.

In the Evening

Blood and Gold, by Anne Rice. Hard to find because the customer asks for "The Story of Marius."

Techie X and I talk about *Teen Titans.*

Spanish grammar books.

Computer workshop schedule.

The Count of Monte Cristo, by Alexandre Dumas, but she hangs up before I can retrieve it.

You, Too, Can Find Anybody, by Joseph J. Culligan.

Don't run!

Local jobs online?

Two twelve-year-old girls: "It doesn't matter. I have ketchup." "No, I have ketchup." Is there something going on in the world I don't know about?

Don't run!

"Sing, Sing, Sing," but she wants the sheet music.

Stuff on Clarence Darrow, particularly Leopold and Loeb.

African dance videos.

Matthew Lesko and grant writing books.

Computer workshop schedule.

No sign-up needed for the Internet: 2 (Getting there)

Thursday, January 29, 2004

In the Morning

There's a pay phone in the lobby, ma'am, where it's really cold.

Books on goal setting for middle schoolers.

My brilliant reference interview concludes with me saying "This one's got some stuff and this one's got other stuff."

FAFSA forms.

Nostradamus books.

Info on our adult literacy programs.

Info on our Spanish language programs.

Classifieds.

State tax forms.

"Romance-mysteries?"

Notarization.

Deader by the Lake, by Doug M. Cummings.

1099 forms.

"Can I check out five books?"

Copier advice.

Collectors' Information Bureau's Collectibles Market Guide & Price Index, and *Hyman's Trash or Treasure Guide to Buyers*, by Tony Hyman.

Space Shuttle, by Dennis R. Jenkins.

ILL forms.

In the Afternoon

Librarian Y wonders about her W2 forms.

Rosa Parks.

Once a King, Always a King, but he'll take any Remundo Sanchez books.

Naughty or Nice, by Eric Jerome Dickey.

Her computer just . . . died.

There's no LaSalle Street in this town, in spite of his assurances.

The local unemployment office has moved. Bastards.

Printer advice, part one (sending it to the server).

What about fish skins? "Everything about 'em."

Lies and the Lying Liars Who Tell Them, by Al Franken, and *Bushwhacked*, by Molly Ivins.

Charles Givens books.

The Vampire Book, by J. Gordon Melton.

She needs that Rosa Parks book again.

Zip code.

"Poems." You need to narrow it down. "What would you recommend?"

Hawaii, the government, and "why it's special."

Computer workshop schedule.

How to draw cartoons.

Sunday's paper.

Flyy Girl, by Omar Tyree.

Supervision of Police Personnel, by Nathan F. Iannone and Marvin D. Iannone, and *Criminal Investigation,* by Charles R. Swanson, Neil C. Chamelin and Leonard Territo.

Company address.

I think someone told someone that we own Kelley books now. We're getting more calls.

Financial aid books.

"Where are the adult nonfiction?"

BMX bikes.

Pencil.

Chaucer.

Poe.

"Do you speak Spanish?" No. "Do you speak Spanish?"

Emily Dickinson

Careers in graphic design, computer animation, that sort of thing.

ESL books.

I curse at my computer a little too loudly.

No sign-up needed for the Internet: 4

Chapter 9

The Library As a Retail Outlet

HOW ONE LIBRARY TRANSFORMED ITSELF INTO AN XPRESS SHOP ·

As a Seattle resident, where one can find two Starbucks within 500 feet of each other, the latest incarnation of the "marketing" approach to public library service, called the "retail" model in some places, is perhaps a logical place to find libraries converting book space to cafés, Wi-Fi centers, plasma-screen entertainment centers, and so forth. I have observed this trend to one extent or another in local libraries, but a small library in Colorado will serve as an example of a true makeover in library orientation and services.

In response to a posting on the PUBLIB e-mail list, Laurie Christensen, Manager of the Castlewood Branch in the Arapahoe Library District (Colorado), was kind enough to share her experiences of changing to a retail approach to library services.

> In an effort to find a niche in the District for Castlewood and increase our usage, we adopted a retail model of library service. This is sometimes referred to as a "destination library," and we coined the term Xpress. We decided to focus on multiple copies of popular best-selling books, DVDs, audio books and magazines. For example, we get twenty copies of *People magazine* each week, anywhere from fifteen to twenty copies of a hot new DVD and twenty to thirty copies of a new best-selling book. All magazines circulate, including the current issues. We have impulse racks at our check-out desk with new magazines. There are no holds and no renewals on Xpress materials. (Christensen, 2004)

Reference Librarianship: Notes from the Trenches
© 2006 by The Haworth Press, Inc. All rights reserved.
doi:10.1300/5672_09

Christensen now refers to the approach as "Xpress Libraries" and says circulation has skyrocketed since the change. She also notes the idea has been picked up by other libraries. Financing the concentration on popular materials of the entertainment variety was made possible by reducing the nonfiction and reference collections.

Of course, concentrating on popular materials is nothing new. For years, Charles Robinson, long-time director of the Baltimore County Public Library, followed this approach (although his critics sometimes misunderstood his idea of popular). If Homer's *Iliad* was popular, Charlie would carry it. I remember some of the (at that time) heretical thoughts to which I was exposed when I first worked in one of his libraries. "No reserves on best sellers!" "Buy forty copies of the same *New York Times* best-seller book for just one branch." "Discard one book every time you add a new one." However, his methods certainly got results, at least as far as circulation went. Although reference was not downplayed per se, Robinson's insistence on generalists rather than specialists (that is, his idea that any librarian should be able to [and did] work both adult and children's desks) did not, at least as far as I remember, make reference the focus of any library. This was mitigated by the presence within Baltimore County of the great Enoch Pratt Free Library, with its outstanding reference services.

What happens to reference services in libraries that take the retail path, attractive and "with-it" as it may be, if they do not have a nearby large library to which to send customers? Many years ago, when automobile gasoline was a lot cheaper, a landmark study claimed that library users were seldom willing to travel more than 1.5 miles to get to a library. Unless an excellent reference referral service exists (which grows ever harder in shrinking library budgets), with reference staff dedicated to using it, customers who find their information needs unmet may leave unsatisfied or simply turn to the Web if they can.

All sorts of questions emerge if a library tries to rely on other libraries for more in-depth reference help, particularly when the backup library is not part of the same taxing district. Christensen is fortunate to have a nearby larger library in her system. In other situations, will customers of similar Xpress libraries have to fall back on Web access for their information needs? If libraries diminish reference collections and staff in order to focus on quick in-and-out service for popular materials, are they serving one element of the population at the expense of another?

Do these questions really matter when articles in the literature suggest that reference use is decreasing everywhere? In local library systems, total reference questions over the past ten years have declined, sometimes by as much as 50 percent, despite area population in that same period growing approximately 10 percent. Circulation continues to grow, as it did at Castlewood, so by this test the approach does seem to meet the circulation definition of success. Perhaps, since so much now is available on the Web, and if libraries can provide sufficient online access for computer-deficient households, this may be the most cost-effective and public-relations-wise approach to take in the coming decade. To popularize this approach, libraries are making more effective use of retail concepts such as branding, marketing, and advertising.

These retail attempts are based in part on the assumption that current publishing and distribution methods will remain relatively stable. Currently, no evidence regarding the way that current modes of publishing operate suggests that doing away with books will be economically viable. Although we certainly are participating in a digital world, and books now are prepared digitally, the major distribution format probably will remain hard copy for at least some time in the future. However, because of the possibilities of electronic reproduction of text, distribution methods may change sooner than we expect. We already see some changes. Online bookstores can get you any book in print in a short amount of time. Other online venues such as eBay and Half.com provide access to long-out-of-print books that formerly required finding and dealing with antiquarian booksellers. Recently, through these latter online services I have with very little effort been able to collect a number of books that sat on my bookshelf as a young teenager. The experience, despite its nostalgic focus, was one that dramatized for me the changes in book distribution made possible by the Web.

Of course, if distribution methods change so that customers no longer have to come to the library to get their reading material, we will have many white elephants sitting around the landscape without the capabilities and staff to mediate between yottabytes of online information and the public, which will need to winnow through that information. Perhaps another vision from 1990 will come to pass:

> Although there are no public libraries per se, the concept of the librarian as a middle-person between stored knowledge and end

user still exists in 2020. However, the library has become an intellectual rather than a physical entity. Many public service librarians made the transition to the National Reading Center (NRC) and now spend their days reading newly published material and crating the digests, reviews, and annotations that allow the general public to make wise choices about reading material. (Anderson, 1990, p. 93)

📖 📖 📖

A GRUNT'S DIARY: FEBRUARY 2004

Sunday, February 8, 2004

In the Afternoon

It's a stampede! The doors open and one minute later all 35 machines are occupied.

Techie X gets a lecture about cars.

They'll issue you a card over there, sir.

Anthem, by Ayn Rand.

Stapler. She breaks it.

Today's paper.

Crit on Shakespeare's sonnets.

There's a dog loose in the library!

Microfilm reader lecture.

Sandra Cisneros.

"Hide your gum!" cries the girl.

Those aren't state forms ma'am, they're federal.

A constitution book in Spanish.

John Gotti.

Reboot.

Pencil.

Out of the stacks, kids.

Pencil.

Lots of Hispanic author guides.

Microfilm reader refresher course.

To Kill a Mockingbird (film).

The kid's section is downstairs, ma'am.

Copier advice.

Hernando Tellez.

Pablo Neruda.

Shakespeare's sonnets again.

Microfilm reader advice.

Today's paper.

Local history.

Printer advice.

Consumer Reports for 2003.

Boxing.

Today's paper.

Check books out over there, sir.

Biographies are over there.

Microfilm reader advice.

Another damn sonnet.

"The interpretation of EKGs."

Stanislavsky.

I nearly step on a kid.

Today's paper, and yesterday's, and a phone book.

Jesse Owens.

Reboot.

Ralph Abernathy.

Frederick Douglass.

"Lady of Spain" for accordion.

"World War I, and religion."

Wal-Mart, and how their lawsuits are going.

Yes ma'am, that number on the spine is the call number. I don't care what your teacher told you.

Maya Angelou.

Local building history.

Library history.

Phone books.

Gabriel García Márquez.

It's five minutes until we close, and no one wants to leave the Internet terminals.

All our SQL server books are checked out. He is not happy.

This is the busiest shift I can remember.

Monday, February 9, 2004

In the Evening

The meeting room is downstairs, ma'am.

She needs a book, at least 250 pages.

1987 Cadillac Brougham repair manual. He settles for a Fleetwood.

Everything about England.

Careers in art.

Jamaica Kincaid. Sorry, no cell phones.

Peaches.

History of a local landmark.

Two notarizations.

Bush's Brain, by James Moore and Wayne Slater.

"Abraham Lincoln was our first president, right?" No. "Who was?" George
Washington. "That's right! Lincoln was the sixteenth!" And off she ran.

"How much to print." He looked suspicious of everything I said.

WPs are over there, ma'am.

"The names of the fingers."

Pit bull books.

Check out books over there, sir.

Divorce books.

Shut up!

Help with printing a too-slick Web page.

No, you can't clip out articles from our newspapers.

Somebody's Angel Child, by Carman Moore.

He needs a pen, and a cigarette for later.

Ask at circ if you need the phone, sir.

She once had a book that had all the religions in the world and when they
started, with a couple pictures of each. But that's all she remembers.

Sorry sir, we don't have that newspaper on microfilm, sir.

Sunday paper.

Citizenship books, and Bible study.

I almost step on another kid.

Large print books.

Affirmative action.

Sorry ma'am, I can't teach you how to use Word.

Another sonnet.

A sheet of legal-size paper.

Pen.

American Jesus, by Stephen Prothero.

Stapler.

The last-minute printing people . . .

No sign-up needed for the Internet: 8

Thursday, February 19, 2004

In the Morning

Driver's ed manual.

Out of Gas, by David Goodstein, and *The Hydrogen Economy,* by Jeremy Rifkin.

Printer advice.

She is delighted to learn we have old papers on microfilm.

"Do you have the books I want?" No, except for *The Big Bounce,* by Elmore Leonard.

Pencil.

Copier advice.

Our WPs don't like his disk.

Beanie Babies books.

She's not sure if she wants box 13 or ballot box 13.

The books are waiting for you at circ, I promise, ma'am. No one else checked them out.

She's excited. All her friends from the shelter are here!

If you want to open a file, sir, stop clicking on "save."

An atlas that contains Indian burial mounds. Cool, but we don't have it.

In the Afternoon

What did you say? A yearbook? Which one? Yes, I know you mean a high school yearbook, I meant what year?

Dictionary.

Aha, no wonder you can't enter your SS number. Your number lock is turned off.

They realize I shouldn't be out here and I get replaced.

In the Evening

Local AA meetings.

Quantum computing.

A small child coughs up a lung.

Writings of Ulysses Grant and Frederick Douglass.

Study room?

Books on animals. She doesn't know what an animal is. She's a grown woman.

Copier advice.

Chocolate for a Teen's Spirit, by Kay Allenbaugh.

The place is loud and packed with teens. Some carry posterboard. A project must be due tomorrow.

No ma'am, you cannot plug your smartcard reader into our machines. Please don't guilt-trip me.

A disturbance at the front door, and cries of "Call the police!" I suppose I had better see what is going on.

Car buying guides.

I leave to conduct a workshop. I come back.

They'll break a dollar at the front desk, kid.

Copier advice.

Luther Gulick? Never heard of him.

Number of times I wanted to throttle a middle-schooler: 18

Monday, February 23, 2004

In the Afternoon

Copier advice.

Copier advice.

Reboot.

Printer advice.

Today's paper.

"The difference between the University of Illinois and Eastern Illinois University."

Would I Lie to You? by Trisha R. Thomas, and *A Hustler's Wife*, by Nikki Turner.

Friday and Saturday paper.

8 Minutes in the Morning, by Jorge Cruise.

Books by Andre Dubus.

"I need the number to the school." Which school, sir? "That's a good question."

Copier advice.

Notarizations, yearbooks, all sorts of stuff all at once until I get free for my workshop.

He wants to put up a flyer for a Bix Beiderbecke tribute. He tears away his coat to reveal a Bix T-shirt like he's Superman in a phone booth. "It's all we talk about!"

Lost notebooks returned.

The bearded man says to the two girls in matching pink coats: "These are the reference librarians. They're the gentlemen you need to speak to today." The girls don't look too sure.

Frederico García Lorca, for the class's South American authors project? Where are these teachers coming from?

Milk in My Coffee, by Eric Jerome Dickey.

Ebony magazine from 1963. Actually all she wanted was MLK's Letter from Birmingham Jail.

Gwendolyn Brooks.

Achondroplasia. The handwriting and spelling is so bad I thought it was another Hispanic author name.

"I can't get onto Yahoo."

Garrett A. Morgan. "He was a black male who invented something."

"Is aluminum pounded steel?"

Pit bulls, or Staffordshire terriers.

Baby names.

A child sharpens a pencil way too thoroughly.

Dostoyevsky.

Yes ma'am, that's scratch paper.

Copier advice.

"I need to write a report on gay people." His friends snicker behind him.

Don't run!

Business plans.

We close at nine, kid.

Holds are at the circ desk, ma'am. No, we're not circ. That's over there.

Stapler.

I kick several kids off the Internet machines.

"The 258s are the sex books," the kid insists.

Printer advice.

Thomas Jefferson.

Mysteries of the Bible.

Animals of Australia.

No eating in the library, sir.

No sign-up needed for the Internet: 12

Wednesday, February 25, 2004

In the Afternoon

Twelve pizzas have arrived.

Computer workshop info.

Get change at the front desk, sir.

The literacy rate in 1890.

The phone number to the solicitor general.

Books on writing.

Copier advice.

Local drivers license bureau phone.

"I have some money to give to Alzheimer's"

Donald Goines books.

January 27 paper.

Today's paper. "I'M TOTALLY DEAF!"

Local Department of Revenue phone.

1937 obituary.

Reporting civil rights 1941-1963.

Stapler.

Reboot.

Stapler.

2001 yearbook.

He whispers "Someone left porn on a machine." His breath is terrible. And the woman wasn't even naked.

Printer advice.

The Five People You Meet in Heaven, by Mitch Albom. She thought it was six people.

Our porn snitch comes back to report another customer. Again, the woman was clothed.

In the Evening

DC-area businesses that make over a million dollars.

Can I help you? "No."

Tax counseling is downstairs, sir.

Phone number to a local parochial school.

No, she wants the phone number to the church that runs the school. Sigh.

Tax counseling is downstairs, sir.

Books on appliqués. She refuses my help.

A book called *Black Year,* but I can't find it anywhere. . . .

Angela Davis and the Black Panthers.

Last Wednesday's paper.

Sigh. Last Thursday's and Friday's papers.

"You Know How to Make Me Feel So Good," by Harold Melvin and the Blue Notes.

2002 newspapers.

"Chesapeake Appraisals" phone number.

Jelly Roll Morton.

Baby names.

Harriet Tubman's family.

My back is killing me.

Amelia Earhart.

Pencil.

No, kid, you can't plug your scanner in here.

Don't run!

To search for the obit, sir, I will need a last name.

Get with the Program, by Bob Greene.

Another whine about our computer policy. My backache is creeping into my head.

Printer advice.

I leave to conduct a workshop. No one comes. I return to the desk.

Left Behind, by Tim LaHaye and Jerry B. Jenkins.

Rubber band.

Online catalog advice.

They'll sell you a disk at circ, ma'am.

The history of Harlem, which leads to a discussion on gentrification.

How to spell "Rosa Parks."

Printer advice. She demands her dime back.

What year did JFK die? She then proceeds to tell me where she was, how the nuns were crying, etc.

Scissors.

The GI Bill, by Milton Greenberg.

No sign-up needed for the Internet: 8

Thursday, February 26, 2004

In the Afternoon

They'll make change at the front desk, ma'am.

"I hit something and it messed it up."

A whine about paying for the copier.

Pencil and paper.

A call wrongly transferred to us.

Copier advice.

"Robert Flemming, who invented the guitar."

Where are today's papers?

Investor's Business Daily.

I hate salesman, so I transfer her to my boss.

I leave to conduct a workshop. I come back.

Today's paper.

A U.S. road atlas he can check out.

Printer advice. Cool Brit accent.

Printer advice. They mess it up and whine for their money.

Our PR person's e-mail.

A list of college radio stations.

Diabetes.

Tax forms.

Stapler.

In the Evening

Hamsters.

Honduras.

The woman at the copier just can't figure it out. She calls out to Librarian Q: "Ma'am? . . . Ma'am? . . . Ma'am?"

A cop tells off a couple of our brattier middle-schoolers, which makes me smirk.

Another Internet policy whine.

The Lost Boy, by Dave Pelzer. Someone left a copy on our counter. The customer is amazed when I pick it up and hand it to her.

Vikings.

Stop hitting each other, kids, or you're off the machines.

They'll make change at the front desk, sir.

I give my microfilm-reader lecture. She calls me by my first name because she read it off my badge. I hate that.

The TV version of *Purlie,* and *Crossfire Trail.*

The Wiz, but the interview is slowed by his belief that the title is "Oz."

A Bible. "Never mind," says the kid.

Mat wrestling.

Typing instruction on CD-ROM.

"Ferraris." Here you are. ". . . Lamborghinis." Let me show you how to use the catalog.

Betsy Ross.

Two teenage boys converge on a tiny screaming girl in the stacks. They carry her off to her fate (the parents).

Practical nursing guidebooks.

Now another teenage boy hunts down another tiny girl. At least she's not screaming.

"Who do I put down as the editor of *Occupational Outlook Handbook?*"

Something about Chrysler being bought out.

She'll settle for just about anyone close to that name living in Las Vegas.

Books by Gordon Fee.

That's not a reference book. You can check it out, sir.

Sorry, we don't give away old newspapers, ma'am.

I hate these four-hour shifts . . .

Chapter 10

Staffing Tomorrow's Library

HIRE FOR THE SMILE, TRAIN FOR THE JOB

Once upon a time in a library long ago, in order to be an excellent reference librarian you needed skills such as a wide knowledge of printed reference sources; an ability to analyze a question into specific types such as encyclopedic, specific fact, source location, or bibliographic; a liberal arts background; and a fantastic sense of curiosity.

In 1990, according to one study, you needed the following qualities (DeVries & Rodkewich, 1997):

- approachability
- curiosity
- empathy
- nonjudgmental
- persistence
- competitive
- logical thought process
- intuitive

When the authors repeated the study in 1996, all of these, with the exception of "competitive," were for the most part still highly rated qualities, although being nonjudgmental did not get as a high a rating as in 1990. However, in 1996 two new traits were added—flexibility and collaborative abilities. Reference was no longer seen as a one-person challenge; rather, working with others was valued because the world of electronic reference was getting too huge for any single approach to work well.

Reference Librarianship: Notes from the Trenches
© 2006 by The Haworth Press, Inc. All rights reserved.
doi:10.1300/5672_10

In the brave new world of twenty-first century reference, judging at least from what one retrieves from a Web search on "reference competencies" plus anecdotal evidence from local library hiring practices, a lot more emphasis is placed on how one relates to the public and the quality of a potential employee's smile. In some cases, the primary competency relates to "approachability." There are a number of variations on the common themes of establishing initial eye contact with the customer, being ready to engage approaching customers, welcoming the customer with a smile and a nice greeting, and so on. However, other libraries seem to focus on "Digital Reference Competencies" relating to technological issues.

This leads to the impression that reference knowledge, as Louis Shores and, later, Bill Katz might have defined it, or even basic library working experience at any level is not considered as important today as are customer-service skills, at least in filling new positions. Hence the title of this section, "Hire for the Smile, Train for the Job." This would seem to represent a new focus on getting people who are outstanding "retail-types," that is, who would probably do well in any retail sales environment, and giving them whatever training the library feels is necessary.

As I pondered these new hiring practices, it occurred to me to wonder whether I could be hired as a new librarian with the MLS degree that I earned in 1969. Out of curiosity, I dug up my transcript from library school. The course content was obvious in titles such as Materials for Adults, Basic Reference Sources, Descriptive Cataloging, Subject Cataloging, Library Administration, Information Resources in the Humanities, and Government Publications. If memory serves, probably no more than thirty or so courses were available in the master's program.

Next, I went to the course descriptions of several graduate library science programs found on the Web. In a number of cases, not only was the list of course offerings two or three times as large as thirty years ago, I had a difficult time understanding from just the title exactly what the course covered because of the use of current high-tech speak. I looked at the descriptions and found fascinating subjects such as:

- Overview of the major concepts, processes and systems, actors, and operations in the life cycle of information.

- Introduction to the user-centered approach to information behavior.
- Concepts, processes, and skills related to parts of the life cycle of knowledge.
- Introduction and overview of information systems, system architectures, and retrieval models.
- Concepts, processes, and issues related to the larger social context within which the life cycle of knowledge is played out.
- Introduction to internal and external management issues and practices in information organizations.

To illustrate how far out of touch I am with the current thinking on information, it came as news to me that knowledge had a life cycle. Was the knowledge of Aristotle past its life cycle? Did knowledge, like radioactive materials, have a half-life as well? I could not find (which is not to say that it is not buried somewhere) a course that taught "Basic Reference Sources." Perhaps basic sources no longer exist—only basic Web sites, although the Reference and User Services Division of the American Library Association still publishes an annual Best Reference Sources list.

Even if somewhere, in either library education or an on-the-job training system, some emphasis is still placed on knowing just what is in various reference sources, I see a troubling point. There would seem to be a logical connection between a public library that wants to position itself as centrally organized around a theme of retail marketing and the consequent need to hire people who are skilled in acting as "greeters" and have the other accoutrements of popular marketing ideas. This provides an interesting, albeit puzzling, contrast with what certainly seems to be a highly theoretical approach to a degree that seems still to be called, at least in most graduate programs, a master's of library and information science. In this case, it seems fair to ask whether new graduates presenting themselves for employment with all of the seemingly esoteric knowledge gained in graduate schools would not be well served to take some additional courses in the business school, or even at a local community college that teaches customer-relations skills.

However, perhaps in libraries and library systems in which reference is being devalued in deference to circulating materials, the primary need might be for both paraprofessionals—the kind of knowledgeable book staff that one finds in major bookstores—and people who in older days would have been called clerks but need a better term now to describe a job that takes care of behind-the-scenes materials handling. The idea of library technicians has been around for decades, although the term as used in the past was often a bit misleading, since sometimes there was not anything really technical about their jobs. Library media technicians once repaired projectors; now library techs may repair computers. Library aides perhaps has too close a connotation to teachers' aides, but bachelor librarians seems a bit odd. Library associate is another well-respected term. The Baltimore County Public Library has had for decades a formal Library Associate Training Program. It is interesting to note that even today current vacancies for librarians at that institution require an MLS from an ALA accredited school, completion of the Library Associate Training Program, or a bachelor's degree and six months of related experience to qualify for a reference desk position.

Who will staff the reference desks at tomorrow's public libraries, assuming there are such desks? Hopefully people with humanistic skills who understand the Machine and can smile while giving service.

📖   📖   📖

A GRUNT'S DIARY: MARCH 2004

Tuesday, March 2, 2004

In the Morning

Printer advice.

More printer advice.

Sorry sir, *Glorious Appearing* isn't out yet.

Baby names.

Where to get a phone book.

The spelling of "tremendously."

Sorry, I can't read our computer workshop schedule over the phone.

Shut up! (several times, to our homeless friends)

Copier advice.

Tax counseling info.

Benjamin's Ghosts, by Gerhard Richter.

Phone number for a local lawyer.

Copier advice.

"They told me to come here to get divorce forms."

Bus lines to correctional facilities.

I fax a computer workshop schedule.

Phone for the local animal control.

Stock quotes from 2003. The man laughs at everything I say.

What kind of file do you need to print, sir?

He did not read a sign, a copier took his money, and he's mad at me.

Pipe fitting.

Everyone seems to think I'm their best buddy today. It's driving me nuts.

In the Afternoon

The Souls of Black Folk, by W.E.B. Du Bois.

The Sixteenth Round, by Rubin Carter.

Someone at circ strangles another baby.

More divorce books.

"Excuse me, sir, I need you to get me started on the Internet."

Today's paper.

"Excuse me again sir, I need you to get me started on the Internet again."

The workshop started at 2. She comes at 2:40 and wonders where everyone is.

An Internet question: "I don't see the car."

The third request for divorce forms today.

Reboot.

Copier advice, or "Sir, come here please."

Psychotherapy East and West, by Alan Watts.

I believe he can't get the Web page to come up because he's never used the Internet. He can barely use a mouse.

Today's paper.

Okay, it's not like the customers think I'm their best buddy today. Rather, they're laughing at their own especially (for a Tuesday) stupid jokes.

Too young for the Internet, kids. "Wait until next year!"

Tax forms are over there, ma'am, and you can download the ones we don't carry.

He's lost the Web site again. I knew this would happen.

Immortal Beloved.

We nearly lose a man's ID.

She tells two girls: "I'm not bringing you guys to the library again."

Front desk will sell you a floppy, sir.

Bodybuilding.

We nearly lose another ID.

Part of *The Wall Street Journal* is missing. He's going to speak to the manager.

He went from "books on religion" to "books that show you that religion is good."

Papers from 1994.

Awakening, by Cate Tiernan. Not *The Awakening,* by Kate Chopin. The customer mumbled a lot.

Egyptian art.

Microfilm reader advice.

Break dancing.

Printer advice.

"I have to write a ten-page paper about Imperialism." And I want to strangle her teacher.

In the Evening

She wants to know how to download and use a program we don't allow.

Seven days of newspapers.

Printer advice.

More printer advice while she tells me how much better another library is.

Real estate law.

General law (different customer).

She has to read a short story for class. Any story. She has no idea.

Librarian Y please come home. Or I'll steal your office supplies.

Thursday, March 4, 2004

In the Morning

Pencil.

Lost disk.

Computer workshop schedule.

Copies are a dime, sir.

Scissors.

How to doublespace.

The margins are already there, ma'am.

For some reason "Print" won't work.

1993 Hyundai repair manual.

Tape.

More printer advice.

More.

And still more.

Baby names.

Stapler.

Physiology.

I turn off his machine and he continues to stare at the now-blank screen.

Yesterday's paper.

Stapler.

Can I check this out?

Magnifying text.

That's a card catalog, sir, not an Internet machine.

The time.

Selling used cars.

A design on a work of cut glass, which he brought and insists on showing to me.

Copier advice.

Novels on Japanese immigration.

Printer advice.

Where's a copier that's working?

A Night to Remember, by Walter Lord.

In the Evening

WPs are over there, sir.

The Source magazine, or any hip-hop periodicals.

They'll break a fiver at circ, sir.

War of the gold-fo? What's that? (The Gulf War)

Printer advice.

Her keyboard stopped working.

Cartas a Ricardo, by Rosario Castellanos.

Shut up, kid (twice).

Cartas a Ricardo, by Rosario Castellanos

My Bloody Life: The Making of a Latin King, by Reymundo Sanchez.

Stapler.

British imperialism. The poor middle-schooler. . . .

Printer advice.

Tax forms are over there, ma'am.

Did she format the line of poetry on her paper correctly?

Jaime Escalante.

I leave to teach a computer workshop. I come back.

Sorry, no fax machine.

Front desk will make change, sir.

Our page is stuck in the elevator!

"Movements of indigenous peoples in Ecuador."

1040EZ

Printer advice.

Librarian Y please come home. We've kept the pile of review mags just as you left them.

Monday, March 8, 2004

In the Afternoon

Librarian Y is back wearing a clever disguise. She has a new perm.

All the information we have on a tiny business in another town.

City directory.

Some old newspapers.

Tax forms.

City directories, lots of city directories.

Books showing that reading improves the mind.

Her document is blank, because it's the wrong one.

Fax machine?

Computer workshop schedule.

Phone book, newspaper, and a whine.

Bus schedules and a funny look. I think he thinks we're hiding some routes from him.

Phone book.

Printer advice.

D. H. Lawrence and Percy Bysshe Shelley.

Komodo dragons.

The Moulin Rouge, by Jacques Pessis

Another library's phone.

Printer advice.

Where the hell's my replacement?

The Death of Innocence, by Mamie Till-Mobley and Christopher Benson.

In the Evening

I can't figure out a trick in Word, but the customers are forgiving.

The Awakening, by Kate Chopin, *A Catcher in the Rye,* by J. D. Salinger, *Jane Eyre,* by Charlotte Brontë, and *Rabbit, Run,* by John Updike.

Printer advice.

Another Word trick, but I solve this one.

Fiction is over there, sir.

Printer advice.

How to recharge a debit card.

Printer advice.

Printer advice.

Prison reform, alternative sentencing, etc.

Another Internet policy complaint.

No ma'am I cannot go around the library looking for a girl in "a white shirt with something red over it." Whining won't help. Neither will guilt trips.

A notarization.

The copier makes change, ma'am.

Bosnia.

No, you can't use the print server to type a paper, sir.

Copier advice.

Stapler.

The Reappearance of the Christ, by Alice Bailey.

Astronomy and wines.

Shut up! Don't fight!

Boolean logic, Venn diagrams, and stuff about, for instance, Max Planck.

Thursday, March 11, 2004

In the Morning

Automatic transmission books.

Consumer legal guides (her automatic transmission died—different customer).

Status of an ILL he requested yesterday.

Book discussion group books for another library.

Building a home bar.

They'll stamp your parking ticket at circ, sir.

He's sitting at a computer and not using it, while others wait. He gets pissed when I tell him to move.

Social Security office.

Local Rotary club.

"Jet books."

Real estate exams.

Book discussion group books for our library.

Computer workshop info.

FAFSA forms.

Does another library have the same microfilm as we do? Do they have their own? And countless other microfilm questions.

Our machines don't like her floppy.

Bathroom?

ASVAB books.

Small business books.

Microfilm printer advice.

"Can you teach me how to work a computer?"

Copier advice.

Printer advice.

"Do you think I can find a career on these Internets?"

Bound Feet and Western Dress, by Pang-Mei Natasha Chang.

Adding an image to her Yahoo! profile.

Math books.

"Business manager salaries?"

State tax form.

Printer advice.

In the Afternoon

Copier advice.

Printer advice.

The Great Gatsby, by F. Scott Fitzgerald (CliffsNotes).

Dream Sewing Spaces, by Lynette Ranney Black.

The Ultimate Weight Solution, by Phil McGraw, *Superfoods,* by Steven G. Pratt
    and Kathy Matthews, and *Audrey Hepburn,* by Sean Hepburn Ferrer.

Our copier/printer rates are going up. I put up signs for the customers to ignore.

Local chiropractor.

Do we buy books for teachers?

She's here to pick up books chosen by high schoolers. Wha?

Kids' section is downstairs.

Whoops, that site isn't too work friendly.

Just press "enter," ma'am.

SARS.

Wahida Clark.

Pictures of the barrier reef.

A middle school teacher calls. It's local history project time again. Oh god.

If the cell phone has to play "Hall of the Mountain King," the least they could do is get the notes right.

Exam proctor question.

Sunday's paper.

History of Barbie.

Microfilm is over there, ma'am.

Johnny Tremain, by Esther Forbes, on audio.

We just started offering fax service today, and already people are calling up and stopping by.

Wednesday, March 24, 2004

In the Morning

"It won't print."

More printer advice.

Scratch paper.

Nursing exam books.

City housing guide.

Lifetime Encyclopedia of Letters, by Harold B. Meyer.

"It won't go to Yahoo. It just sits there."

Computer workshop schedule.

ASVAB books.

"How do I erase all this stuff?"

Books on photography and prostrate cancer.

"I want to print out my credit report."

Fax.

Sunday, March 28, 2004

In the Afternoon

The doors open. God, it's like a swarm.

WPs are over there, ma'am.

Ida B. Wells.

Area parks.

Local history books.

Why is her brother in jail, and why did another guy have his green card "deported?"

Saturday's paper.

Printer advice.

Weekend paper.

"How do I look for jobs on the Internet?"

Runaway Jury on DVD.

Today's paper.

The only available Zane book is the one she doesn't want. We do better with Omar Tyree.

Books by Queen Afua.

Play Piano in a Flash, by Scott Houston.

Nah, your computer isn't frozen, sir.

Snakes, at least that's what he claims to want when I spot him lounging in the stacks with his buddy, pulling out books at random.

Plants, so his buddy claims.

Monet.

Wuaw-wuaw-wuaw-wuaw-wuaw-wuaw-wuaw, says the boy, over and over and over. I finally go over and tell him to shut up. "My sister was about to throw bread."

He doesn't ask. He just takes the stapler.

Dona Nobis Pacem, by Ralph Vaughan Williams.

Today's paper.

"What are your hours today?"

Google is one of many search engines, sir. You don't have to use it.

1040 EZ

Typewriter? Sorry, not here.

Chicken Soup for the Teenage Soul II, and those Pelzer books.

Is "Imparse" a word (though she doesn't know the actual spelling, let alone the meaning)?

Printer advice.

Monday, March 29, 2004

In the Afternoon

Stapler.

Law library phone number.

Computer workshop info.

Printer advice.

There's an online catalog right over there, sir.

The Two-Income Trap, by Elizabeth Warren and Amelia Warren Tyagi.

Today's paper.

When is spring break?

Copier advice.

Cold Sassy Tree, by Olive Ann Burns.

Real estate exam books.

A kid's librarian hands me something to throw away.

Just press enter, ma'am.

In the Evening

Every public computer develops its own unique problem at once.

Biographical sketches of Condoleezza Rice, Colin Powell, and Jesse Jackson.

Sorry, ma'am, your daughter is too young to use the Internet terminals up here.

"My computer's broke." Sigh.

Copier advice.

"The printer won't . . . er . . ."

Dandelion Wine, by Ray Bradbury.

Printer advice.

3-hole punch.

"My computer is saying it'd like to do an illegal operation."

Printer advice.

Printer advice.

"Mumble-mumble-mumble-pen?"

My Bloody Life, and *Once a King, Always a King,* by Reymundo Sanchez.

Newspapers last week, for an obit.

U.S. road atlas.

"Can you hold this for me while I'm in the bathroom?"

This customer is going to keep asking us for tax advice until we wear down.

More newspapers.

"Something is wrong with that computer."

Printer advice.

Sorry sir, they don't let me renew ILLs.

They'll sell you a floppy at the front desk, sir.

"Can you hold this for me again?"

Copier advice.

Chapter 11

Building Tomorrow's Library

WHY DID I TELL YOU I WAS GOING
TO SHANGHAI?

The title of this section bears about as much relationship to the subject matter as some new library designs bear to probable needs of libraries in the coming decades. However, the song, a 1951 Doris Day hit, does deal with misunderstandings. As the singer says, "It was just a little misunderstanding." Some cities and other governing agencies that control public libraries may suffer from little misunderstandings when they decide to build a new library. It some cases, it seems management has turned over the design of new libraries being built today to the wildest flights of architectural imagination available without any real awareness of likely coming developments in the delivery of library services.

In a classic non-rocket-scientist thinking mode, is it not obvious that the way people use public libraries has gone through some dramatic changes—which are far from over? Paraphrasing one longtime librarian's thoughts:

> No one, unless retired, has the time for leisurely gathering of information for information's sake—"the University of the Mind" approach. They do have time to use the library for specific how-to information: sell bonds, plant daffodils, retrain for a new job, write a resume, purchase a camera, for current fiction and nonfiction, for unabridged audio books (because they are too expensive to buy individually), for travel planning materials and for genealogical research. Finally, they use it for their kids, because more and more folks actually are recognizing the importance of reading in the early years. (Anderson, 2004)

Reference Librarianship: Notes from the Trenches
© 2006 by The Haworth Press, Inc. All rights reserved.
doi:10.1300/5672_11

Now match these uses with the type of descriptions found in the annual survey of new libraries in *Library Journal* or in the fulsome praise found in local newspapers after the opening of new multimillion dollar urban libraries:

- "Focuses its Lens, a five-story atrium . . . iron filigree entryway . . . high ceilings incorporate open ductwork . . . has a rainforest theme and stained glass . . ." (Fox, 2003, pp. 47-48).
- "Designed to place roughly 75 percent of the library's collection in accessible, open space . . . [with] a continuous . . . ramp, four levels in height. . . . Some critics thought the spiral concept defied gravity, common sense and safety. . . . You'll love it if you're in a wheelchair (Muschamp, 2004).

Regarding the last comment, it seems a parenthetical note could have been added to the effect that the wheelchairs should have good brakes. Also, can one buy book trucks now with brakes? When I contrast these architecturally magnificent and expensive buildings in city centers with their probable attendant problems of customer access (parking, bus routes, and so on) with the Xpress service concept described in Chapter 9 and its extremely flexible and accessible design, I have to wonder which approach will best serve the users ten to twenty years from now. In other words, does it make sense anymore to build libraries that are monuments for urban pride or would it be better to design smaller, open buildings with less restrictions on change that are located in neighborhoods where the customers live?

Let us ask some more questions:

- In five to ten years, will people go to the local library for answers to the kinds of questions that made reference work so challenging over the past decades?
- As budgets shrink and staffing costs rise, how long can extremely large libraries continue to serve the public? Years ago, some prescient library planners were maintaining that the maximum cost-effective size of a library was 50,000 square feet.
- If the main business of public libraries in the next few decades becomes the delivery not of specific information (let the Web do that) but rather of hard copy books and other media, then which approach is more efficient—a centralized monument that may be difficult to get to—or a warehouse with a local distribution

system? The latter model of course would mean a move from many independent libraries to larger affiliated networks of libraries. However, this model would match other consumer services that rely more on providing needed elements "just-in-time" from distribution centers rather than building enormous edifices that may become difficult to staff, where materials sit on the shelves "just-in-case" of need.

Out of 104 new public libraries listed in the 2003 *Library Journal* review, sixty-eight were branch libraries. Of the remaining thirty-six, only five exceeded 50,000 square feet and only three fell into what I would call the behemoth size. All of the super-size libraries seem to be architectural masterpieces. Nevertheless, I have to wonder how they will fare—what people will think of them ten years from now should change proceed as it has been. Of course, given the remarkable equanimity with which many library customers accept what they are given, maybe no one will remark on future difficulties. It reminds me of an old story about a visitor to a Maine lobster farm watching workers throw live lobsters into boiling water and complaining about the cruelty. After thinking about it a moment, one worker said, "Oh, but they are used to it."

Fortunately, most library users are used to and very forgiving of the big things such as twenty-million-dollar cost over-runs, or thirty-five million dollar service centers, while complaining only about small exigencies, such as a downed wireless network or reserves not showing up.

In many ways, the problems that architects may or may not solve effectively rests with the idea expressed by Louis Sullivan that "form follows function." This elementary idea, simple on the face of it, has given birth to countless architectural and philosophical discussions that delve into such ideas as whether function actually can exist before form or does function refer to actual functioning or intended functioning. Although I am neither an architect nor a philosopher, I would apply Ockham's razor and reduce this issue to its simplest terms as applied to designing new library buildings. No one wants to build yesterday's library. Given that today's library almost certainly will not be tomorrow's library, how does one design for the future?

Not, I would suggest, by designing buildings that ignore probable developments in libraries. Libraries are certainly not exempt from technological change. They will continue to feel the effects of the ever-growing amount of information available online, in more and more complex networks, and in a global information environment. As one writer pointed out, "Technology has become the essential disrupter of markets and operating models. Technology, in other words, isn't the solution. It's the problem" (Downes, 1997). How libraries will deal with tomorrow's operating market models will determine the success or failure of the entire public library system as we proceed into the twenty-first century. In part, this success or failure may well rest on the types of buildings we are putting up today. At best, one can only design the most flexible of spaces that can easily be changed to other purposes without exorbitant structural remodeling costs. If the result happens to look beautiful and win awards, fine, but the more important result is that it work as well tomorrow as it does today. Looking at the marvelous new buildings, particularly the ones that run into the multimillion, or even six-figure costs and appear each year, one can only hope that behind these glorious facades there lurks not only current utility but an adaptability to change.

📖   📖   📖

A GRUNT'S DIARY: APRIL 2004

Thursday, April 1, 2004

In the Morning

The Omega-3 Connection, by Andrew L. Stoll.

No ma'am, switching from '98 to XP isn't that hard.

Reboot.

Book discussion group info.

Where to find Air America locally.

Printer advice.

Obits from way back.

How to get a debit card here.

Info on an old vocational school that used to be downtown.

Fax.

Nearby library's phone.

Sharpening Made Easy, by Steve Bottorff.

Some child custody form 2-1401. "They said the library has it."

In the Afternoon

Today's paper.

Naughty or Nice, by Eric Jerome Dickey.

She doesn't have time to download her tax form.

Books on Word.

Another tax form.

Yesterday's paper.

Yesterday's *Wall Street Journal.*

Roman Italy, by T. W. Potter, and *Romans on the Bay of Naples,* by John H. D'Arms.

1993 Chevrolet Cube Van repair manual.

He left all his tax stuff with the tax counselors, and now they're gone.

Stapler.

That's not an Internet terminal, sir. That's a card catalog.

Another old man at a loss with the Internet and expecting an instant class.

More impatience with our obviously incompetent Internet policy.

Copier advice.

There's an online catalog you can use, sir.

I go to a pointless, depressing meeting. I come back.

Copier advice.

The Zone, by Barry Sears.

Press enter, sir.

The kids' section is downstairs, sir.

Stamp price guides.

Louis Armstrong.

1040X

Computer workshop schedule.

"Strong black novels, like Martin Luther King. You know: war. African-Americans. Race. War books . . ." This is an adult speaking.

Monday, April 5, 2004

In the Evening

Sunday's paper.

The Barefoot Contessa Cookbook, by Ina Garten.

Once a King, Always a King, by Reymundo Sanchez.

On the Down Low, by James L. King and E. Lynn Harris.

Copier advice.

Bathroom?

They'll break a fiver at the front desk, sir.

Bathroom?

Notarization. They ask me what the form is all about. I have no idea.

Reboot.

Debit card use lecture.

And another.

"Do I put the card in this way?"

The House of Dies Drear, by Virginia Hamilton.

GED books.

Reboot.

Off the machine, kid.

"Do you have a cart to put books we have pulled?"

Five kids at one Internet terminal, doing an inmate search. "He got six years." "Naw, he got four."

Phone book.

Mozart's 40th on a cell phone ringer just isn't the same.

Books on the *Titanic*.

Printer advice.

Reboot.

Control-Alt-Delete twenty times.

Heart of Soul, by Elina and Leah Furman.

I download a state tax form.

A college guidebook I can't locate.

Family Portrait Photography, by Helen T. Boursier, and *Location Portraiture of Families and Executives,* by Van W. and Pam C. Frazier.

Voter registration.

Printer advice.

Faulty debit card.

How to send an attachment.

Printer advice.

Insomnia.

Malcolm X.

Copier advice.

Books on Crystal Reports.

Tuesday, April 6, 2004

In the Morning

Today we introduce a new Internet use policy. They must have a library card. They get one hour. This is in response to our no ID needed, unlimited time policy, which was a disaster, with many, many complaints.

Less than a minute into the shift I get my first complaint about the new system, a lady who lost a few minutes because of a printer snafu: "You mean you can't give me extra time after your incompetence?"

Just as we expected.

Fax.

1991 Dodge Spirit repair manual.

We're out of the state 1040s so we print them out on demand.

Notarization.

Stapler.

State 1040.

Notarization.

Local map.

Religious education books and videos.

You can get a library card at the front desk, ma'am.

Pain Free, by Pete Egoscue with Roger Gittines, and *The Power of Now,* by Eckhart Tolle.

Sure your bar code works, sir. Let me show you. . . .

Local genealogical society contact info.

We have a new Internet system, sir or ma'am: 11

Tuesday, April 13, 2004

In the Morning

Fax.

Copier advice.

Lies Women Believe, by Nancy Leigh DeMoss, and *A Short Guide to a Happy Life,* by Anna Quindlen.

Multiple printer advice.

Special Internet.

Someone's phone number.

Virginia Beach jobs.

A giggling senior citizen finds a "risqué image" (manga drawing of a girl) on her computer.

Criss-Cross.

Printer advice.

They'll look up your barcode at the circ desk, sir.

I leave the desk for a pointless meeting. I return.

Restroom?

Phone number look-up.

"Can I leave two kids in the children's section while I do a cover letter?"

You need a library card to use the computers, sir.

Blood and Oil, by Manucher Farmanfarmaian, *Daughter of Persia,* by Sattareh Farman Farmaian, and *Desert Queen,* by Janet Wallach.

"I need the estimated forms."

Type your barcode there, sir: 6

Thursday, April 15, 2004

In the Morning

"I logged into a WP by mistake."

Computer Friendly, by Raymond Steinbacher.

A staff member wanting an ILL butts into line.

"My computer froze."

State tax form.

"How do I get an e-mail address?"

"How do I open this file?"

A sob story about how he needs his taxes done.

Her resume spills onto two pages because of spaces and she doesn't want to pay.

Address to Scholastic, Inc.

The spelling of an Italian word she cannot pronounce.

There is no state EZ form, sir.

Mayor's office phone.

Another state tax form.

Sorry ma'am, we have no more pens to give out.

Microfilm machine lecture.

You want another copy of the state form? The copier's right over there, ma'am (She pouts).

Fax.

Alderman? City council member? She doesn't know what she wants.

He wants 4868, the form for filing late.

State form.

State form. Just one. More whining.

For the last time, ma'am, they have no aldermen in that town, and state representatives don't deal with unwanted pets.

Where to send her tax forms.

4868.

In the Afternoon

City directories '75, '85, '95.

The printer is offline.

I don't know what form you need, sir.

You need to get a library card to use the computers, sir.

Any local cell-phone company whatsoever.

Yes, ma'am, we still have a few state forms left.

"It won't print."

4868.

Bathroom?

You need a library card blah blah.

Librarian Y plans her herb garden.

Reboot.

State form.

You live in town? Get a damn library card!

Correction fluid.

Emily Dickinson.

Local American Family Insurance offices.

Books on writing picture books, at least that's what I think she wants.

Copying costs $.20, sir.

FIC is over there. PBK FIC is over there.

Astronomy magazines.

You're too young.

Black Hawk Down, by Mark Bowden.

We can't open that file on these computers, sir.

Hamlet, by William Shakespeare, for a brain-dead kid.

Copier advice. He's blowing up an image for a tattoo.

"Bullies . . . gangs . . ." When I show her the books she adds "intolerance."

"Race . . . you know, racist . . . and gangs."

CliffsNotes for *Nectar in a Sieve,* by Kamala Markandaya.

"Do you have a list of people who survived the Holocaust?"

I think a lot of school assignments are due next week.

Reboot.

Fiction is over there, ma'am.

New Internet system, sir or ma'am: 12

Thursday, April 22, 2004

In the Morning

A lot of printer advice for three different customers.

I sign up two "guests" for the Internet.

One of our pages gets a phone call that really pisses him off.

Zane and Eric Jerome Dickey books.

More printer advice.

Word advice.

Much more general computer advice.

You need a library card to use the computer, sir.

Tax counseling phone number.

One Hundred Years of Solitude, by Gabriel García Márquez, and *The Heart Is a Lonely Hunter,* by Carson McCullers.

Quilting.

Yes, ma'am there are plenty of Web sites for job hunters.

City directory.

Morningstar.

Computer workshop schedule.

Older city directories. I then need to show her how they work.

Resume books.

"I'd like to use the Internet."

Deaths in Africa because of AIDS.

Local newspaper articles from 1998.

Librarian Y goes home sick but I think she just wants to miss a meeting.

Computer workshop schedule.

Type your barcode in there, sir.

Reboot.

Type your barcode in there, sir.

In the Afternoon

Type your barcode in there, sir.

Stop calling me by my first name, sir.

The Web page he wants is taking forever to load, but I can't help him.

A liver transplant video.

The meanings of "plight" and "dilemma."

Today's paper.

How to play a conga.

GED books.

How many seniors are there in the United States, and how many of them are on Medicare?

You need your library card to use the Internet terminals, ma'am. No, you can't use your kid's.

Night, by Elie Wiesel.

The spelling of "reoccur."

Reboot.

Printer advice.

Reboot.

You can pick up holds at the front desk, ma'am.

Kids Around the World—Cook! by Arlette N. Bramam.

In that case you'll need to get a new library card, sir.

He's looking for his niece, who ran away two weeks ago.

I reset a print server.

The Bermuda Triangle.

I reset a print server while others butt into line.

Baseball's Great Dynasties: The Cubs, by Thomas G. Aylesworth. It makes no sense to me, either.

I reset a printer.

Reboot.

Newspapers going back two weeks.

You gotta be high school age at least to use the ones up here, kids.

Reboot.

I reset a printer.

The Mermaid of Cafur, by Evelyn Foster.

Two final reboots.

Saturday, April 24, 2004

In the Morning

I reset the printer.

The yellow pages she is using does not include churches.

Local phone number.

You need your library card to use the Internet, sir.

Ditto, ma'am.

Birth certificate from Panola County, MS.

The Drama of the Gifted Child, by Alice Miller.

You need your library card, sir.

And ma'am.

A customer approves of our new Internet system. Later, another customer steals his online session.

Once again the copier is smarter than the customer using it.

Pencil sharpener.

"How old is this Web page?"

A Walk on the Beach, by Joan Anderson.

Morning devotionals.

Books on publishing poetry.

Volcanoes.

Reboot.

Life During Wartime, by Keith Reddin.

"A book called *Mister Landlord.*" Actually she wanted *The Landlord's Kit,* by Jeffrey Taylor.

Using a paper clip I rescue a library card from the floppy drive. The customer is both embarrassed and grateful.

Reboot.

Scratch paper.

Yes, we have PowerPoint. No, we don't have a scanner.

Biographies?

The status of an ILL.

Reboot.

Reboot.

You need a library card, ma'am.

Today's paper.

Printer advice.

Al Capone.

One Hundred Years of Solitude by Gabriel García Márquez, and *The Heart Is a Lonely Hunter,* by Carson McCullers.

Lengthy help for a half-blind customer who is unfamiliar with the Web and wants a site I can't locate.

Videos on segregation.

Don't run!

Kids' section is downstairs, kid.

In the Afternoon

How to do two-sided copies on the glass.

A textbook. The customer keeps calling me by my first name.

Textbook.

Local shelters. "We got nowhere to go and we're just walking around and around . . ."

Key of Knowledge, by Nora Roberts.

Reboot.

Sorry ma'am, those are the only shelters we know about.

Reboot.

Twice he has come to the desk, placed the almanac he borrowed on the counter, changed his mind and walked away. He also does it with his ID card.

He calls to make sure we have books on photography, and Mark Twain.

No sleeping in the library, sir.

Microfilm reader lecture.

Reboot.

Not all of Adobe Acrobat's print buttons work. Annoying.

How to save on a floppy.

Local art classes?

Literary criticism of *A Midsummer Night's Dream*? You already found them. Yes, ma'am, the books you are holding have literary criticism. Good job!

Just walk over and type your barcode, ma'am.

True, he is a regular. He had no library card, and he wants to play Internet chess. He acts like I'm a close friend. I say no. So much for our beautiful friendship.

Form 9465.

Every couple months I get a craving for Eno's *Another Green World.* I sneak downstairs to get it.

We look and look but can't track down a Comiskey Street in Chicago.

Wednesday, April 28, 2004

In the Morning

Printer advice.

King, Warrior, Magician, Lover, by Robert Moore.

Printer advice.

That Bach tocatta as a cell-phone ringer.

Quilting.

Don't run!

City directories.

Info on the Alpha Kappa Alpha sorority.

More city directories.

Talk to circ, sir.

His ILL is messed up. He wanted a GED CD-ROM, not a book.

Ebony back issues.

You need a library card. . . .

Type your barcode there. . . .

Repeat.

Printer advice.

Scholarship books that she can check out.

Today's paper.

Bus schedule.

Something about maps. I wasn't paying attention.

That's a pdf form, ma'am. You can't fill it out online.

A services directory.

Reboot.

Copyright forms.

Books by David Bach.

Origin of the quote "'Tis a far, far better thing . . ."

In the Afternoon

Books about Myra Cohn Livingston. "She's not American. She's from New England."

Does she want *Baby Mama Drama,* by Russell Bailey, or *Baby Momma Drama,* by Carl Weber? She has no idea. She'll take them both.

Just type your barcode in, ma'am.

Just type your barcode in, sir. Oh. Then you better talk with circ.

Do we have any lectures coming up on women and gender? She was just hoping . . .

He gets offended that he needs a library card to use the computers now.

"You got any CDs of romantic orchestral?" They finally decide on Wagner. Heh heh.

Edna St. Vincent Millay.

Fax.

An adult starts an Internet session and immediately leaves. A minute later a kid jumps on the machine.

Four giggling middle schoolers and one six-year-old want volcano books.

Julia Alvarez.

Reboot.

WPs are over there, sir.

She looks asleep, but one finger is tapping.

Reboot.

I can't help you until I finish helping her, sir.

Reboot.

Of course you can use that online catalog, sir.

Local history. How many wards?

I get thanked for something. I forget what.

Lit crit on *Frankenstein*.

Down syndrome and F. Scott Fitzgerald. Not together.

You need a library card, ma'am.

Stapler.

There's a working copier near the front door, sir.

Chapter 12

How Did We Get Here
from There?

WHERE DID WE GO WRONG/RIGHT?

This will not be a review of the history of the public library movement in the United States since 1826, when the idea first floated in
Boston. I will not even get into the "modern" history described by
Patrick Williams, when the doors of a rented schoolhouse opened to
the public on March 20, 1854 (Williams, 1988). Rather, I want to talk
about one person's experience with public libraries, beginning with a
flashback to the 1940s and then hopping forward to present time.

From the time that I began visiting the local library in a small suburb of a large city, I checked out four books every two weeks. I read
widely, if not with great discrimination, about the French and Indian
Wars, American air aces of World War I, submarine heroes of World
War II, Gobi desert archaeology, taming wild animals, Toussaint
Louverture, and John Carter of Barsoom (I had to buy the latter
books; I suppose they did not fit the library's collection-development
policy). As far as I can remember, I never used a card catalog. I browsed.
This was the exciting part of a library visit—wandering down the
aisles with the knowledge that possibly a new adventure might await
me on the next shelf. When I discovered a new author, I read more
books by that person. This was a single library, not part of a network,
so what I could find was limited to one location. This never seemed to
be a shortcoming. To a child's eyes then, the reading possibilities in
even that small library seemed endless. I did not need a summer reading program—even if one had existed. What pleasure is greater than
stretching out in a tree house on a long summer day reading tales of
other lands, even other worlds?

Reference Librarianship: Notes from the Trenches
© 2006 by The Haworth Press, Inc. All rights reserved.
doi:10.1300/5672_12

Now my local library is a branch of a large urban library system. A hundred or so books are on the new-fiction shelves and perhaps twice that many on the new-nonfiction shelves. The older materials are a hodgepodge of books published over the past thirty years or so. With luck, between the new section and the old, I can usually find four books every two weeks. I do not know whether it is a judgment on the quality of new publications or simply more discrimination on my part, but I usually end by giving up on one or more of these after the first chapter.

However, public access computer catalogs are available that, if I can find one unused by someone surfing the Web or checking e-mail, will let me order any one of several million books owned by the library system. This request system is well used. An entire small room at my branch is dedicated to books awaiting pickup by requesters. It seems that one of the changes that have taken place over sixty-odd years relating to users' available time, as noted in "Why Did I Tell You I Was Going to Shanghai?" is a focused approach to library use rather than the old browsing approach. Somehow, this method loses some of the excitement of wandering through shelves. Even with the most sophisticated of Web catalogs that include book reviews, it really is not the same. In libraries, the French tagline of *plus ça change, plus la même chose* no longer applies.

Things have changed. That little individual library in the 1940s had about 22,000 books, and the annual budget for materials, staff, and operations was about $26,000. The 2003 budget of the library system to which my local branch belongs was $29,559,529 and the total holdings were in excess of two million volumes. My local branch has around 60,000 volumes and spends more than $650,000 on staff alone. Circulation in my childhood library averaged around 112,000 per year with a per capita circ of 17.23. My large library system circulation is over six million a year from the central library and twenty-three branches. The per capita circulation is 11.15. Compared to my little library of the 1940s, my large library system now checks out about fifty-six times as many materials to a population base that is about eighty-six times as large. However, the budget for this current library system is 1,137 percent larger than my 1940s library. During the period under comparison, the Consumer Price Index increased roughly 560 percent. To put it another way, the 2004 budget of my current library system would equal $2,837,715 in 1944 dollars or 109 times the budget of my little library of the 1940s.

Just two more statistical comparisons will finish my points here. The turnover rate (total circulation divided by volumes owned—a simple measure of collection use) is 3.51 for my big library system. In my little old library, it was 5.1. This huge library system, therefore, has about ninety-two times more materials that get about 30 percent less use than the library of my youth. Finally, that little library I have described in such nostalgic terms spent 42 percent of its budget on salaries. The large library system of which my current branch is a part spends about 74 percent of its budget on salaries. Of course, it is a different world now than it was in the 1940s. It probably is statistically unfair to compare a library in a small, relatively affluent suburb to a huge library system in another state, but still, the differences resonate with me.

I suspect the greatly increased needs of specialized staff to deal with all the technological innovations that exist in libraries today, as well as the costs of computerization, account for some differentials over and above the simple effects of inflation. What is the public buying with all of these new services? Access is probably the word that first comes to mind. The user is not limited to the collection of a small, nearby library, nor does the user have to try to find a parking place at a large downtown library built to serve a half million people that has only 200 parking spaces. Home access to the library's Web pages is available. Without leaving my computer, I can request any one of the two million books in the system (excluding reference, lost items, and so on). I can borrow CDs, videos, DVDs, and whatever the newest medium of publication happens to be. I can get access to multiple databases whose cost would be prohibitive to an individual. One of these databases alone is so expensive that a nearby library system, with an even larger budget ($72 million) can afford only three simultaneous users—once every month or so in the dead of night, I can log on to this database!

Why, then, given this richness of resources, is it harder to find something decent to read on a library visit? Now I have to be on the alert by checking review sources, including an e-mail updating service, for new titles and then rush to put a reserve on interesting books—getting on a list with 642 other people before me.

As discussed in Chapter 3, technology has a revenge effect. Public libraries sixty years ago did not have the purchasing options that libraries now have. It was pretty much books and some magazines in those earlier days. Now, if one surveys nationwide library statistics, many libraries are doing very well if they are able to spend 15 percent of their budget on books. As far as a reading public is concerned, are we better off now than we were then? The U.S. Post Office once spent $356 million in one year on automation. Then they had to hire additional staff to deal with the new technology. If you pay considerably more (Express or Priority), you can send things faster through the mails, but is first-class mail delivery any better than it was sixty years ago? What did all that technology buy? At least one-fourth of the time, our mail is delivered to the wrong house! If reading is fundamental, why does only about fifteen to twenty cents of every library dollar go to buying books?

Is there perhaps a subconscious element that drives librarians (or at least library administrators) to focus on ever newer technological toys, not just in the belief that this is what the public wants but also to shore up the public's perception of librarians as not only "Professionals" but also as "Masters of the Machine?" Obviously, there is no going back, and I am sure few would want to return to those glorious days of yesteryear. In the next ten years, though, as costs and availability of electronic access increases, what will our public library look like?

A standard definition of the word *library* is a place set apart to contain books for reading, study, or reference. This connection with books exists from early times, when Romans used the bark of a tree (liber) as a writing material. Chaucer, in 1374, used this language in *Boethius:* "The walles of thi lybrarye aparayled and wrowht with yuory and with glas" *(Oxford English Dictionary Online)*. This is perhaps an apt description of the brand-new downtown library where I live. However, with the changing role and content of libraries, it seems to me that we had better start trying to think of a better word to describe this place that holds more and more computers and less and less books, because the old meaning may not have a connection with the reality of the future.

📖   📖   📖

A GRUNT'S DIARY: MAY 2004

Sunday, May 2, 2004

In the Afternoon

You need a library card to use the computers, sir.

Charles Dickens.

No Bob Dylan, ma'am. I think you mean Dylan Thomas.

WPs are over there, sir.

Printer advice.

All our copiers are broken ma'am.

Medical dictionaries.

"Biographies of the Alamo."

Anne Sexton.

Spanish books.

Pencil.

Milwaukee phone book.

The printer ate his money.

Pencil.

Don't run!

Last week a cell phone did the "tocatta" part. Today another phone plays the "fugue" part.

Food pyramid on the Internet.

Reboot.

Don't run!

The Great Gatsby, by F. Scott Fitzgerald.

I reset a printer.

The girl comes in for *Gatsby,* but circ can't find where I put it.

Today's paper.

Reboot.

You need a library card, ma'am.

Don't run!

Don't run! (sigh)

I reset a printer.

That's the call number there, sir, and biographies are over there.

Capital punishment, books, and two magazine articles please.

You can get a replacement card at the front desk, sir.

The Communist Manifesto, by Marx and Engels.

Printer problems and a reboot.

Don't run!

Press the print button, lady.

You didn't save your work? I have bad news for you.

Printer advice.

Reboot.

Kurt Vonnegut.

I show her how to get to the online databases a second time.

Sorry, sir. The public terminals shut off automatically ten minutes before closing. Nothing I can do.

State tax form. She has a terrible cough.

Times I say "Just type in your barcode": 11

Monday, May 3, 2004

In the Morning

The copy machine downstairs still works, sir. . . . Whoops, no it doesn't.

City directory.

Black Girl Lost, by Donald Goines.

Sugar Busters, by H. Leighton Steward et al.

They'll look up your number at the front desk, sir.

Avascular necrosis.

1997 Plymouth Voyager repair manual.

She needs a librarian who can speak Spanish.

Phone number to a church.

Phone number for a cab.

State tax form.

I log in a guest Internet user.

Math books.

Mexican weddings and Catholicism.

Computer workshop schedule.

Shut up!

Printer advice, twice.

Sidney Sheldon books.

I said shut up!

In the Afternoon

I relieve Librarian Y, who is muttering to herself. I think she had a busy shift.

Printer advice.

Reboot.

You need a library card to use the Internet, sir.

I say it again, to a different customer, who is not happy with me.

Reboot.

Reboot.

Reboot.

Paul Laurence Dunbar.

She's looking for a quiet corner at 3:50 in the afternoon during the school year. Ha ha!

Printer advice.

Those machines over there have CD-ROM drives, sir.

Mary, Queen of Scots.

1993 Chevrolet Caprice repair manual.

"Poetry of John Updike." Also Billy Collins.

She can only narrow it down to "A Hispanic-American woman poet."

The old man says, "You sure changed things around here."

Reboot.

Carl Sandburg.

Sandra Cisneros.

Emily Brontë.

How to get to another library catalog.

Emily Dickinson.

Edgar Allen Poe.

Smart Women Finish Rich, by David Bach, and *Mortgages for Dummies,* by Eric Tyson and Ray Brown.

Harlem Renaissance.

Reboot.

Reboot.

Tape and scissors.

You need a library card, ma'am.

Reboot.

You can't use that paper in our printers, sir.

The computer isn't messed up, ma'am, the Web page is.

We close at nine, sir.

You can go downstairs without having to check out those books, sir.

Federico García Lorca.

Bathroom?

Reboot.

Reboot.

Times I gave the library barcode speech: 4

Tuesday, May 4, 2004

In the Evening

Sorry, ma'am, you can't take the newspaper out of the library.

Sorry, ma'am, we have no place for you to leave flyers.

Today's paper.

How to copy legal size.

Puerto Rico and Mexico.

Gays and the church.

You need a library card, ma'am.

Reboot.

You pick up books at the circ desk, kid.

Street gangs.

India.

Matthew Lesko books.

Much advice on A: drives, networks, and printers. I don't think the customer understood a word.

Microsoft and ADO and Access. He keeps staring at us even after we've shown him everything.

Tiling, then bathrooms, cabinets, and dry wall.

The computer guy still won't go away.

"Can I draw pictures on Microsoft?" (Not the computer guy)

"Will you sharpen this pencil for me, please?"

Printer advice.

Pre-GED math videos.

Two reboots, a lost document and a saved one.

Phone number to Soldier Field.

Apes, for her grandson. Happily the kid shows up and narrows it down to Orangutans.

Surely I'll hold onto this copy of *Poet's Market* for you, if you give me your phone number (I didn't really say that).

The Jacket, by Andrew Clements.

Wednesday, May 5, 2004

In the Evening

"Where's this?"

How to save.

"Drugs." I think he's on them.

"I thought the copier was a change machine and it ate my dollar."

JFK.

Your session is over, sir.

Type your barcode there, ma'am.

Fiction is over there.

"Music." Can you narrow it down? ". . . Music."

"I'm going to need assistance with the computer."

Printer advice.

Eloise Greenfield.

Legal books.

Reboot.

Human resources development.

I reset two machines.

Computer workshop schedule.

Maya Angelou.

"Can I see this pencil?"

Maps of Europe in 1914.

Another reset.

Newspapers from April.

Manatees.

That's not an Internet terminal, ma'am. That's an online catalog.

I repeat the above for another customer.

Randall Jarrell.

His images are too big to fit on his BlackPlanet profile.

I wish Acrobat would stop trying to upgrade itself.

Pictures of jazz instruments.

Ourselves to Know, by John O'Hara. The customer goes on about how he's a distant relative.

LSAT books.

Word advice.

Lots of whining because she can't find her card.

Oedipus Anne, by Diana Hume George, and *Anne Sexton,* by Diane Middlebrook.

I am told our new computer system is a ripoff.

I reset the printer.

He's lost his ID and other stuff. . . . No he didn't.

Nuts! by Kevin and Jackie Freiberg.

South Beach Diet books.

Thursday, May 6, 2004

In the Morning

Yup, you need a library card to use the computers.

I say it again.

Sigh, and again.

Yes, we have some 1880s newspapers on microfilm, sir.

"When's the next Harry Potter book coming out?"

Type your library barcode there, sir.

"You gotta help me on the Internet because I'm kinda legally blind."

You need a library card, sir.

In the Afternoon

"I need the phone number to Microsoft Word."

The Coldest Winter Ever, by Sister Souljah.

Today's paper.

He's worried that he performed an "illegal operation." I reassure him. Meanwhile, another customer barges ahead of him. "Where are the sports books?"

You need a library card, ma'am.

Paralegal careers.

Just type your card number there, ma'am.

She can't get the VH1 page to load.

Thursday, May 13, 2004

In the Morning

State tax form. Two copies.

They'll look up your barcode at the front desk for money, sir.

Our accountant borrows our copy of *Morningstar,* which troubles me somehow.

All you need to do is type your barcode in, ma'am.

Consumer info for lawn mowers.

City directory.

Madame C. J. Walker.

How to Fight Cancer and Win, by William L. Fischer.

She works on her document for nearly an hour and doesn't bother to save it. . . .

Project Management for Dummies, by Stanley E. Portny.

Reset fails. Time to reboot. She is convinced computers hate her in particular.

How to get a library card? Wrong desk.

Newspapers we don't have on microfilm.

"Books on ancient battles. Troy and Spartacus."

1040 instructions.

The PC doesn't like his barcode. Whoops, it does now.

Type your barcode there, ma'am.

Their Eyes Were Watching God, by Zora Neale Hurston, and *The Adventures of Huckleberry Finn,* by Mark Twain.

Two more reboots.

In the Afternoon

I smell burning plastic . . .

City directory.

A credit union asks us to do a Criss-Cross.

Two reboots.

Books on the Forties.

Type your barcode in there, sir.

Books on the 1940s.

Sunday's paper.

Stuff about Jack Horkheimer and comets. I google "Greetings, greetings, fellow star gazers." Then he wants to know all about snoezelen.

Shut up!

Reset.

Friday, May 14, 2004

In the Morning

Texas Sunrise, by Fern Michaels.

Type your barcode in there, sir.

Herbal supplements.

You need a library card to use the computer, sir.

A missing insurance card is found, left on the copier glass.

Type your barcode . . .

Our online databases won't work. . . .

You need a library card . . .

Type your barcode . . .

Worse Than Watergate, by John Dean.

I don't know why Amazon's "one-click ordering" isn't working for you, sir.

No cell phones, sir, at least when you talk as loud as that.

Fax.

In the Afternoon

Notarization.

"Biblical Counseling."

Type your barcode . . .

In Evil Hour, by Gabriel García Márquez, *Open Your Mind and Be Healed,* by Johnnie Coleman, and the latest Oprah book.

The Two Babylons, by Alexander Hislop.

Carpentry books.

Type your barcode . . .

How to attach a file.

The computer's just slow, sir. There's nothing I can do.

"Books to teach motivation."

Yesterday's and today's paper.

Copier advice.

Reboot.

You can't use your own paper in the printer, sir.

Reboot.

Type your barcode . . .

Type your barcode . . .

You need a library card . . .

Conclusion

Some of the preceding essays may have appeared to take a dim view of some trends in public library service—almost to the point of seeing the current library world on the "dark side." The reader may have observed more than one nostalgic glance at what I apparently perceive as a golden age of reference services. However, just because one can miss a way of operating in the past (a way that is not yet totally gone, as many of the questions in the diary entries prove) does not mean that bright and shining new ways of doing business have not arrived or are not on the verge of implementation. So much remains to be done in the areas of textual and speech recognition, imaging and imaging retrieval systems, remote delivery of library information, and other as yet unenvisioned enhancements, that we will be limited only by our imaginations—and perhaps a financial constraint here and there!

The possibilities for information retrieval on a scale not even dreamed of ten years ago, not just at the beck and call of trained reference librarians but available to every person with access to the Internet, presages a glorious future. The somewhat hackneyed phrase, "information wants to be free" is, because of the Internet, becoming a truism. Information, despite government attempts to control it, is being exchanged in myriad ways through the Web—from lengthy self-publication efforts to daily blogs on every imaginable subject.

Forward-thinking library directors are recognizing these changes and taking exciting steps to take advantage of new technologies. Jamie LaRue, Director of the Douglas County Public Libraries (Colorado) is embarked on a paradigm-changing remaking of his libraries. Writing in a local newspaper column about changes his users will see in the near future, LaRue posed a number of questions, a few of which are reproduced with his permission (LaRue, 2004, p. 30A):

Reference Librarianship: Notes from the Trenches
© 2006 by The Haworth Press, Inc. All rights reserved.
doi:10.1300/5672_13

- Suppose that instead of having library staff barricaded behind those desks, we were roaming all over the place, maybe with headsets that let us instantly summon expertise from all over the organization—including our crackerjack online reference librarians.
- Suppose that our computers let you not only do e-mail and search databases, but also request notifications of unknown but upcoming titles, or new electronic articles, on topics of interest to you.
- Suppose that our catalog told you about these new options by sending a message to your Palm Pilot or cell phone, just as you stepped through our doors.
- Suppose your local library was THE place where teenagers came to find high-end workstations, enabling them to engage in intense multi-player computer games.
- Suppose that library hours started to look like your own life?

LaRue ended his column by noting that, "we have a choice: we can be victims of change, or we can be agents of improvement."

It is this hope, this choice, that almost makes me wish I were just starting out again on a career in whatever new word might be coined to describe the twenty-first-century role of our profession—a word that should encompass all the many new services and paradigms that our *libraries* are in the process of becoming.

References

Ahern, Mary Eileen (1904). Reference work with the general public. *Public Libraries* 9(February 1904), 55, quoted in Patrick Williams, *The American public library and the problem of purpose* (New York: Greenwood Press, 1988), p. 30.

Anderson, Charles R. (1990). Using technology. *Wilson Library Bulletin,* March, 92-93.

Anderson, Charles R. (1996). An examination of the reference interview using the dynamics of Kierkegaardian existentialism. *RQ,* Fall, 67-71.

Anderson, Charles R. (2003). *Puzzles and essays from 'The Exchange': Tricky reference questions.* Binghamton, NY: Haworth Press.

Anderson, Mary Jane (2004). E-mail message to author, October 26.

Bolter, Jay David (1991). *Writing space: The computer, hypertext, and the history of writing.* Hillsdale, NJ: L. Erlbaum Associates.

Bolter, Jay David (1994). Authors and readers in an age of electronic texts. In Sutton, Brett (Ed.), *Literary texts in an electronic age: Scholarly implications and library services* (p. 7). Urbana-Champaign: Graduate School of Library and Information Science, University of Illinois at Urbana-Champaign.

Christensen, Laurie (2004). Personal communication.

DeVries, JoAnn & Patricia M. Rodkewich (1997). Master reference librarians for a new age: A study of characteristics and traits. In Mabry, Celia Hales (Ed.), *Philosophies of Reference Service* (pp. 206-212). Binghamton, NY: The Haworth Press, Inc.

Downes, Larry (1997). Beyond Porter. *Context,* Winter. Retrieved February 2, 2006, from http://www.contextmag.com/archives/199712/technosynthesis.asp.

Fox, Bette-Lee (2003). These joints are jumpin'. *Library Journal,* December, 40-49.

Ju, Anne (2002, May 30). In search of the green PC. *PC World.* Retrieved February 23, 2006, from http://www.pcworld.com.

Katz, William (1992). *Introduction to reference work.* New York: McGraw-Hill.

LaRue, Jamie (2004, Octorber 27). It's time to rethink what you know about libraries. *Douglas County News-Press,* p. 30A.

Mabry, Celia Hales (2001). *Doing the work of reference: Practical tips for excelling as a reference librarian.* Binghamton, NY: The Haworth Press, Inc.

Microsoft Encarta (2004). *Reference library.* CD-ROM. Redmond: Microsoft Corporation.

Muschamp, Herbert (2004, May 16). The library that puts on fishnets and hits the disco. *The New York Times.* Retrieved February 23, 2006, from http://www. nytimes.com.

Oxford English Dictionary Online. Available at http://dictionary.oed.com.

Pruitt, Scarlet (2004, May 20). Gartner: Replacement cycle expected to spur PC shipments. *Computerworld.* Retrieved Febraury 2, 2006, from http://www. computerworld.com/managementtopics/management/itspending/story/ 0,10801,93297,00html?from=story_picks.

Tenner, Edward (1997). *Why things bite back.* New York: Vintage Books.

Williams, Patrick (1988). *The American public library and the problem of purpose.* New York: Greenwood Press.

Index

Note: The reader should be aware that index entries leading to *Diaries* pages in many cases offer a précis to the more unusual reference desk interactions rather than promise much additional information. In the *Diary* pages, some subjects, such as "Computer crashes," "Printer advice," or "Internet sign-ups" occur so frequently that they are not separately indexed. In these cases, a cross reference directs the reader to *A Grunt's Diary* pages, meaning those masochistically interested in pursuing these perennial annoyances simply can scan the daily entries. Finally, page numbers followed by an i refer to illustrations.

Reference Librarianship: Notes from the Trenches
© 2006 by The Haworth Press, Inc. All rights reserved.
doi:10.1300/5672_15

Order a copy of this book with this form or online at:
http://www.haworthpress.com/store/product.asp?sku=5672

REFERENCE LIBRARIANSHIP
Notes from the Trenches

_____in hardbound at $49.95 (ISBN-13: 978-0-7890-2947-8; ISBN-10: 0-7890-2947-2)

_____in softbound at $24.95 (ISBN-13: 978-0-7890-2948-5; ISBN-10: 0-7890-2948-0)

249 pages plus index • Includes illustrations

Or order online and use special offer code HEC25 in the shopping cart.

COST OF BOOKS_____

POSTAGE & HANDLING_____
(US: $4.00 for first book & $1.50
for each additional book)
(Outside US: $5.00 for first book
& $2.00 for each additional book)

SUBTOTAL_____

IN CANADA: ADD 7% GST_____

STATE TAX_____
(NJ, NY, OH, MN, CA, IL, IN, PA, & SD
residents, add appropriate local sales tax)

FINAL TOTAL_____
(If paying in Canadian funds,
convert using the current
exchange rate, UNESCO
coupons welcome)

☐ **BILL ME LATER:** (Bill-me option is good on US/Canada/Mexico orders only; not good to jobbers, wholesalers, or subscription agencies.)
☐ Check here if billing address is different from shipping address and attach purchase order and billing address information.

Signature_____

☐ **PAYMENT ENCLOSED: $**_____

☐ **PLEASE CHARGE TO MY CREDIT CARD.**

☐ Visa ☐ MasterCard ☐ AmEx ☐ Discover
☐ Diner's Club ☐ Eurocard ☐ JCB

Account # _____

Exp. Date_____

Signature_____

Prices in US dollars and subject to change without notice.

NAME_____

INSTITUTION_____

ADDRESS_____

CITY_____

STATE/ZIP_____

COUNTRY_____ COUNTY (NY residents only)_____

TEL_____ FAX_____

E-MAIL_____

May we use your e-mail address for confirmations and other types of information? ☐ Yes ☐ No We appreciate receiving your e-mail address and fax number. Haworth would like to e-mail or fax special discount offers to you, as a preferred customer. **We will never share, rent, or exchange your e-mail address or fax number.** We regard such actions as an invasion of your privacy.

Order From Your Local Bookstore or Directly From
The Haworth Press, Inc.
10 Alice Street, Binghamton, New York 13904-1580 • USA
TELEPHONE: 1-800-HAWORTH (1-800-429-6784) / Outside US/Canada: (607) 722-5857
FAX: 1-800-895-0582 / Outside US/Canada: (607) 771-0012
E-mail to: orders@haworthpress.com

For orders outside US and Canada, you may wish to order through your local sales representative, distributor, or bookseller.
For information, see http://haworthpress.com/distributors

(Discounts are available for individual orders in US and Canada only, not booksellers/distributors.)

PLEASE PHOTOCOPY THIS FORM FOR YOUR PERSONAL USE.
http://www.HaworthPress.com   BOF06